T0291197

Applied Corporate Risk and Liquidity Management

Applied Corporate Risk and Liquidity Management

ERIK LIE

OXFORD
UNIVERSITY PRESS

OXFORD
UNIVERSITY PRESS

Oxford University Press is a department of the University of Oxford. It furthers
the University's objective of excellence in research, scholarship, and education
by publishing worldwide. Oxford is a registered trade mark of Oxford University
Press in the UK and certain other countries.

Published in the United States of America by Oxford University Press
198 Madison Avenue, New York, NY 10016, United States of America.

© Oxford University Press 2023

Library of Congress Cataloging-in-Publication Data
Names: Lie, Erik, author.
Title: Applied corporate risk and liquidity management / Erik Lie.
Description: New York, NY : Oxford University Press, [2023] |
Includes bibliographical references and index. |
Identifiers: LCCN 2022029617 (print) | LCCN 2022029618 (ebook) |
ISBN 9780197664995 (hardback) | ISBN 9780197665015 (epub)
Subjects: LCSH: Cash management. | Corporations—Finance. |
Financial risk. | Risk management. | Corporate governance.
Classification: LCC HG4028.C45 .L54 2023 (print) |
LCC HG4028.C45 (ebook) | DDC 658.15/244—dc23/eng/20220714
LC record available at https://lccn.loc.gov/2022029617
LC ebook record available at https://lccn.loc.gov/2022029618

DOI: 10.1093/oso/9780197664995.001.0001

1 3 5 7 9 8 6 4 2

Printed by Integrated Books International, United States of America

Contents

Acknowledgments

Sofie Lie and Eloy Sanchez-Vizcaino Mengual provided illustrations, and Richard Peter provided helpful comments.

1

Introduction

Cash holdings play a critical role for all corporations. They serve as a source
of funding for investment projects that create value for shareholders and as
a cushion against costly financial distress. Indeed, the major premise of this
book is that cash deficiencies are costly (e.g., because investments suffer),
and I will refer to these costs so often that I have adopted a term for them that
I use later: *ripple effect*s. But cash holdings can also induce wasteful spending
and attract unwanted attention from labor unions, activist investors, and
politicians. Thus, a secondary premise is that excess cash can be costly.

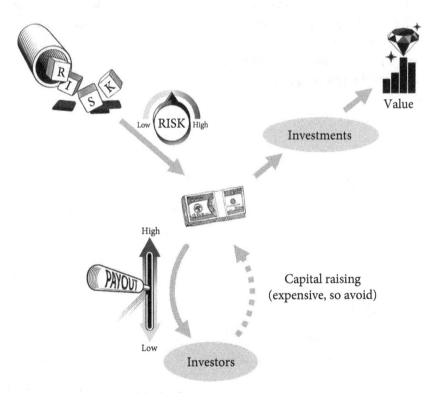

Figure 1.1 Overview of the book

Applied Corporate Risk and Liquidity Management. Erik Lie, Oxford University Press. © Oxford University Press 2023.
DOI: 10.1093/oso/9780197664995.003.0001

Based on these premises, the obvious goal becomes to ensure that the corporation has sufficient—but not excess—cash holdings, both now and in the future. We will explore at length how risk management and payout policies can help attain that goal.

Figure 1.1 shows a simplified framework for the book. The cash balance is at the center of the diagram, feeding the investments that are needed to create value. For the most part, we will take investment opportunities as given, in the sense that the net present value (NPV) of a firm's potential projects is beyond the firm's control. Furthermore, we will try to avoid the external capital market, because raising funds externally is generally quite costly, especially if the firm is already financially squeezed. That leaves only two ways for us to control current and future cash holdings: (1) risk management, that is, the extent to which we mitigate the effect that various risk factors have on operating cash flow and cash holdings; and (2) the payouts we make to investors. Consequently, the figure has a switch for the risk level and a lever for the payout level, but no other way for us to influence the value creation process.

Of course, the real world is more complex than the figure depicts. Thus, we will go further when necessary, for example, by discussing various types of risk, the limitations to managing risk, how risk might affect the NPV of potential projects, and different types of payouts. For now, just remain patient and we will eventually get there.

2

Optimal Cash Holdings

2.1 Cash holdings

In general, we define cash holdings as any liquid investments, including the following:

- cash and cash equivalents: cash and highly liquid investments with a maturity less than three months.
- short-term investments:
  - o financial assets with a maturity of 3–12 months and potentially longer that the firm might sell early to satisfy liquidity needs;
  - o the assets are relatively less liquid, but earn a higher yield, like treasury securities and highly rated corporate and municipal bonds.

However, firms use these categories rather loosely and often include securities that are both risky and illiquid in either category. Thus, we should take the cash and short-term investment categories on firms' balance sheets with a grain of salt, as we should do with many other accounting items.

Furthermore, firms carry financial assets in their long-term investments that could be categorized as cash. A prominent example is that of Apple, which has carried most of their "cash" as long-term investments during the last decade or so.

Figure 2.1 shows the cash and cash equivalents and short-term investments among public non-financial US corporations for the fiscal years 1990 through 2020. The ratios are calculated as aggregate cash and cash equivalents or aggregate short-term investments scaled by aggregate assets. Firms are partitioned into terciles based on size, where size is measured by book value of inflation-adjusted assets.

Applied Corporate Risk and Liquidity Management. Erik Lie, Oxford University Press. © Oxford University Press 2023.
DOI: 10.1093/oso/9780197664995.003.0002

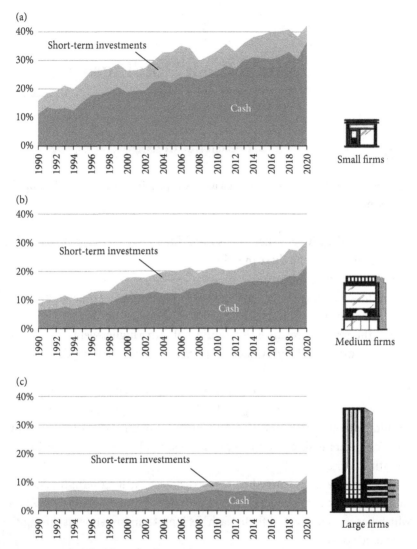

Figure 2.1 Cash holdings by firm size

There are several trends worth noting:

- Cash holdings have increased dramatically in recent decades.
- Small firms hold a much larger portion of their assets in the form of cash than large companies. In fact, small firms kept as much as 40% of their assets in cash and short-term investments in 2020.
- As expected, short-term investments fell in value during the 2008 financial crisis, but the cash balance did not.
- The cash balances increased substantially during the pandemic in 2020.

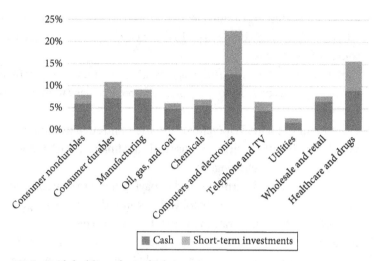

Figure 2.2 Cash holdings by industry

Figure 2.2 displays the cash and cash equivalents across industries. The computer and healthcare sectors, both of which face a lot of uncertainty, have the largest cash balances, whereas the much stabler utility sector has the lowest cash balances. Thus, an uncertain business environment appears to contribute to higher cash balances.

What about lines of credit—is it a substitute for cash? While firms might tap into credit lines for additional liquidity, credit lines come with covenants and can be withdrawn precisely when the firms need them the most. That is, only "cash is king," and will be there for companies irrespective of the circumstances, like your BFF (best friend forever).

2.2 Benefits and costs of cash holdings

There are several sensible reasons for firms to hold cash. Let us start by listing these, and then we will return to many of them later:

i. Cash holdings allow firms ready access to funds for investments. Because investing in positive net present value (NPV) projects is critical for creating value, this is one of the major benefits of cash, and it even forms the basis for an extended example later on why firms engage in risk management.

ii. Cash holdings reduce fundraising costs. Raising funds externally, for example, by issuing equity or debt, can be very costly, especially when the firm is struggling or outside investors are skeptical about the operations and prospects of the firm. In those cases, cash is a much cheaper source of funding.

iii. Cash holdings serve as a cushion against adverse shocks and potential financial distress costs. This is the so-called precautionary motive, to use a buzzword.

iv. Cash holdings can make potential customers and suppliers more willing to do business with the firm, because cash and financial slack serve as signals of firm quality and longevity.

v. Retaining cash inside firms instead of paying it out to shareholders can curb the tax burden for shareholders, because dividends are generally taxed at a relatively high rate in the year they are received.

vi. Retaining cash overseas avoids repatriation taxes associated with bringing the cash back home, which might be necessary to disburse it. In fact, one might argue that any cash overseas should be excluded from a firm's liquidity measure, because it is so costly to bring back overseas cash.

However, cash holdings can also be detrimental:

i. Cash holdings generally generate a low return.[1]

ii. Cash holdings might induce wasteful spending by management, for example, on corporate jets, lavish headquarters, and value-reducing acquisitions.

iii. Cash holdings might make the management and the organization "fat and lazy," because with an abundance of financial resources, the incentive to work hard and streamline operations is weaker.

iv. Cash holdings might attract the attention of labor unions that fight for higher wages for the employees.[2] They can also attract unwanted attention of activist shareholders who favor higher payouts and politicians who push for more investment and higher wages.

---

[1] However, if the cash is invested in, for example, Treasury securities or other liquid securities, it would likely still show up as cash on the balance sheet, and it would generate adequate return given the low risk. That is, investing in Treasury securities is a zero NPV decision, and, as such, neither creates nor destroys value. Related to this, a common argument is that cash is just idle, and, as such, helps neither the company nor the greater economy. This is not quite right. For example, cash that is deposited in a bank account generates interest for the firm, and the bank lends the money to other firms that need capital for investments.

[2] Of course, higher wages are not necessarily bad for the company if it helps retain and recruit good employees. But unions might fight for above-market wages if they believe that firms can afford it and might initiate a strike if cash-rich firms refuse to give in to union demands.

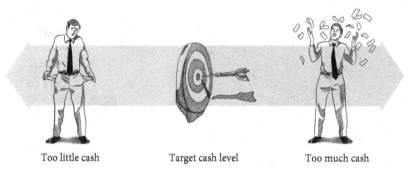

| Too little cash | Target cash level | Too much cash |

Figure 2.3 Cash trade-off

2.3 Trade-off theory of cash

The benefits and costs above give rise to a *trade-off theory*, in which we weigh the benefits and costs of cash holdings, much like you might have seen for capital structure. Such a trade-off implies that firms have an optimal cash level that is neither too high nor too low (the story of Goldilocks comes to mind here), sometimes referred to as the target ratio. This is depicted in Figure 2.3.

2.4 The value of cash

The trade-off theory further implies that one dollar of cash is not necessarily worth one dollar to all firms. On the one hand, for firms with less cash than optimal, one incremental dollar is worth more than one dollar, because they are likely to forego good investment opportunities or incur distress costs. This explains why cash-strapped firms are willing to incur substantial transaction costs to raise funds or sell assets at fire-sale prices. On the other hand, for firms with more cash than optimal, one incremental dollar is worth less than one dollar, because such firms are prone to overinvestment, that is, waste the cash on bad projects. The old idiom of *throwing good money after bad* comes to mind.

Figure 2.4 illustrates this concept. If one dollar of cash is always worth one dollar for a firm, the relation between the cash level and equity value should be a line with a slope of one in the graph. More likely, the relation can be depicted by a concave curve, which is steeper than one for low cash

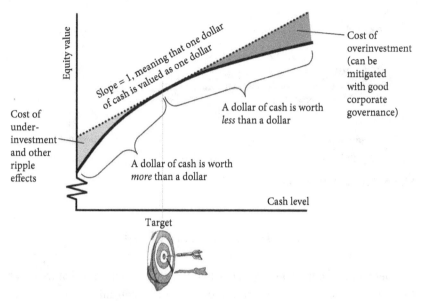

Figure 2.4 The value of cash

levels (meaning that one dollar of cash is worth more than a dollar) and less steep for high cash levels (meaning that one dollar of cash is worth less than a dollar). The degree of concavity on the low end depends on the firm's cost of underinvestment (e.g., what good investment opportunities it has), while the degree of concavity on the high end depends on the inclination to waste cash on bad projects. This is a perfect segue to the effect of corporate governance.

2.5 The effect of corporate governance

Corporate governance refers to the mechanisms by which corporations are monitored and controlled. Good governance mechanisms, such as a strong, informed, and independent board of directors, are critical when managers are tempted to take actions that benefit themselves instead of the corporation. The quality of firms' governance structure affects all kinds of corporate policies and actions. Naturally, it also plays a role for cash holdings, both for how much cash firms hold (versus spend) and for how investors value that cash.

There are two theories for the effect of corporate governance on cash holdings. One is that managers inherently want to accumulate cash to live "the easy life," without the worries of having enough funds when needed. Thus, firms with poor governance are predicted to end up with excess cash. Another theory is that managers gain utility from spending cash, for example, on acquisitions, and are inclined to quickly spend whatever cash the firm generates. (This is why I am careful to not give my kids too much cash when I lack oversight of their spending.) Thus, firms with poor governance are predicted to end up with less cash than optimal. The empirical evidence on these theories is mixed, that is, it is not clear whether poor governance results in more or less cash in practice, and it probably varies from firm to firm.

In either case, we should be concerned when firms with poor governance carry much cash, and the value of such cash is likely to be lower. By contrast, we do not have to be so worried about large cash balances if the firm has strong governance mechanisms that ensure that managers do not waste the cash on bad projects. Thus, good governance helps prevent the investors from discounting the value of excess cash. In Figure 2.4, this would be reflected with a smaller shaded area for high cash levels.

2.6 Competing theories and cash adjustments

An alternative to the trade-off theory is that chasing the target cash level is secondary to other objectives of the firm, such as raising new equity when equity is overpriced or minimizing transaction costs by using cash as a source of financing for new projects instead of external funds. But this *dynamic* view and the trade-off theory are not mutually exclusive. Combined, they imply that firms might optimally deviate from their target ratios.

Yes, I know that it seems contradictory to say that it can be optimal to deviate from the target ratio, especially because I just referred to the target ratio as the optimal ratio when discussing the trade-off theory. What I mean is that the trade-off theory suggests that there is an "optimal" level that balances the costs and benefits of cash, but the competing dynamic view distorts this notion of optimality. From this point on, I will be careful with my wording and use the term *target ratio* when referring to the cash level that balances the costs and benefits under the static trade-off theory.

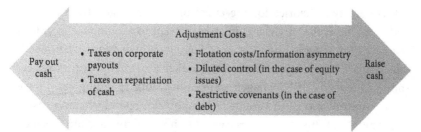

Figure 2.5 The costs of adjusting cash levels

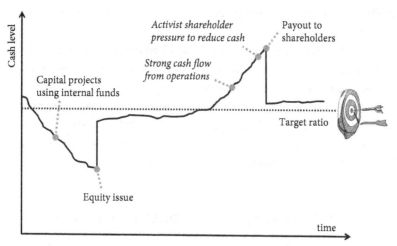

Figure 2.6 Hypothetical cash evolution

The speed at which firms close any gap between actual and target cash levels depends on the relative importance of the two views of cash-level formations as well as the costs of adjusting the cash levels, including taxes on payouts and flotation costs when raising cash, as shown in Figure 2.5. If the trade-off theory is important to managers and the costs of adjusting the cash level is low, the adjustment speed should be high.

Figure 2.6 shows the hypothetical cash evolution for a company. In this example, the target ratio is constant, but it might also vary, for example, as the riskiness of the business environment changes. The firm depicted in the graph apparently allows the cash level to deviate from the target ratio depending on the level of the operating cash flow, but it makes cash adjustments if the deviation is sufficiently large. In practice, the decision to adjust the cash level toward the target ratio is often prompted by the following:

- Pressure from activist shareholders. For example, a shareholder might exert pressure on the company to pay out what it considers to be excess cash, with the goal of raising the company value.
- Changes in the cost of raising funds. For example, if managers perceive the shares to temporarily be overvalued, the managers are more likely to issue shares, because the effective cost of raising equity is lower.
- Changes in the cost of disbursing funds. For example, the government might reduce the dividend tax or the tax of repatriating cash from overseas, in either case effectively reducing the cost of payouts from shareholders' perspective.

2.7 The costs of insufficient cash ("ripple effects")

The trade-off theory suggests that there is a target cash level, or, put differently, there are costs to both insufficient cash and excess cash. Furthermore, the costs and difficulty of adjusting the cash levels imply that firms could get stuck with the costs of insufficient cash or excess cash for prolonged periods.

The costs to insufficient cash are at the core of this book. In fact, they are the underpinning for why firms should engage in risk management in a later chapter. They even play an important role for payout policy, in addition to the costs of excess cash.

What are the costs of insufficient cash then? The earlier discussion on the benefits of holding cash already alluded to these costs. But I have found that it is not sufficient to just list these costs; we need to gain a solid intuition for what they are, when they arise, and why they create such havoc.

All else equal, most people agree that less cash is worse than lots of cash. Moreover, the reason for low cash is often poor cash flow, which we all agree is undesirable. But what led a firm to having insufficient cash, irrespective of whether it is rising costs or large dividend payments, is not the cost of having insufficient cash. The costs of insufficient cash are the costs that arise once the firm finds itself in the situation of having insufficient cash. Did I lose you there?

It might help to first consider cash-strapped individuals. Such individuals cannot afford to buy a house, so they must rent, even if it is cheaper over time to buy. They might have to rent furniture, which is undoubtedly very expensive in the long run. They cannot buy in bulk at Costco, so they pay double at a nearby grocer or convenience store. They cannot buy health insurance, so they pay a much higher medical cost than insurance companies have negotiated if they get sick. They must take up pay-day loans from loan sharks that charge enormous interest rates. Clearly, this is a vicious cycle. James A. Baldwin put it succinctly: "Anyone who has ever struggled with poverty knows how extremely expensive it is to be poor."

Let us consider the decision of renting a house versus buying more closely. Renting a property in a poor neighborhood can be surprisingly costly, both relative to renting in a nicer neighborhood (where landlords are less concerned about getting their rent, having to initiate evictions, and seeing the property ruined or stripped) and to buying the property outright. For example, I have seen estimates of price-to-rent ratios of 50 in San Francisco (meaning that a property that rents out for $1,000 a month would sell for $1,000 × 12 × 50 = $600,000) but only 6 in poverty-ridden Detroit (meaning that a property that rents out for $1,000 a month would sell for $1,000 × 12 × 6 = $72,000). Figure 2.7 illustrates these ratios. Even lower ratios are evident in the poor areas of Milwaukee based on the Pulitzer Prize-winning book *Evicted: Poverty and Profit in the American City* by Matthew Desmond (2016). It seems that buying a house in a poverty-ridden area rather than renting represents a positive NPV, in that an initial investment is very low compared to the savings in future rents. But if you are poor, you must forgo this positive NPV opportunity because you lack the initial equity to buy, and, thus, you are doomed to rent. Individuals with the worst credit record cannot even rent an apartment and might stay in extended-stay hotels at outrageous prices.

Cash-strapped companies experience analogous costs. Their borrowing costs are exorbitant, if they can borrow at all. They might be unable to fund their investment projects, even if they have a positive NPV (we call this *underinvestment*). Their customers and suppliers are getting nervous and might be less willing to do business with the company, perhaps unless the terms for doing business (e.g., prices) are changed. They might sell assets at fire-sale prices. And, worse yet, they might default on debt payments, which spurs all kinds of financial distress costs, including legal expenses.

I like to compare the initial negative cash flow shock that gave rise to the low cash holdings as the initial splash when a waterdrop falls into a glass of water or you throw a rock into a lake, and the subsequent costs

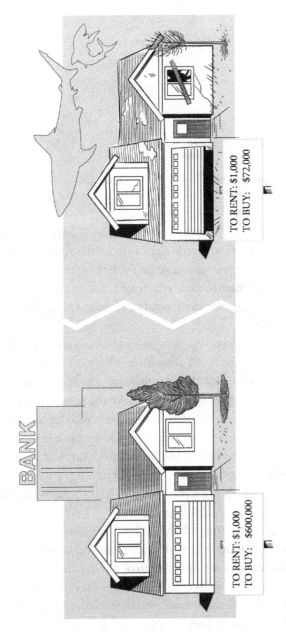

TO RENT: $1,000
TO BUY: $72,000

TO RENT: $1,000
TO BUY: $600,000

BANK

Figure 2.7 The cost of renting vs. buying

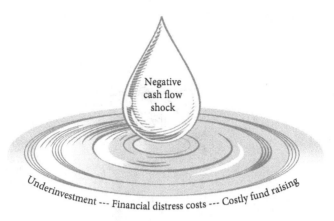

Figure 2.8 The ripple effects of a negative cash flow shock

of insufficient cash as the subsequent ripples, as illustrated in Figure 2.8. Thus, I refer to the costs of insufficient cash as the *ripple effects* (also referred to as *market imperfection costs* or *friction costs* in the risk management literature). The name *ripple effects* underscores that we refer to the consequences of having low cash, not the reasons for having low cash in the first place.

Of course, not all negative cash flow shocks will cause ripples. If a firm has substantial cash holdings, it can absorb negative cash flow shocks without missing a beat. But if the cash drops sufficiently, the ripples start to surface. At what cash level the ripples appear is not clear and naturally depends on the company, for example, to what extent customers consider the financial viability of the company when purchasing its products. But it is generally safe to conclude that *negative* cash levels trigger various costs, and in most parts of this book, we will focus on instances in which the cash level turns negative, that is, instances in which firms run out of cash (because, while cash can be negative in our models, in reality it cannot).

What is relevant then is the probability that firms will experience the ripple effects, or for simplicity, the probability that firms encounter cash deficiency. This obviously depends on not only the current cash balance, but also the uncertainty in future cash flow. Figure 2.9 illustrates the role of uncertainty. The two distributions have the same averages, but the distribution with the larger standard deviation is more likely to have very low values, and, thus, more likely to trigger ripple effects.

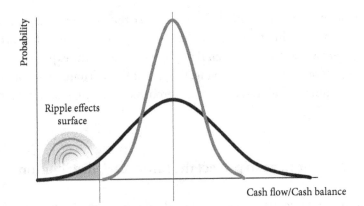

Figure 2.9 Cash uncertainty and ripple effects

2.8 Which companies exhibit the greatest ripples?

There is great variation in the extent to which firms suffer when facing a cash shortage. Some of the important determinants include the following:

- Investment opportunities: Firms with great investment opportunities suffer more from cash shortages because they might have to forego some of those opportunities. A high P/E ratio is a reasonable indicator of good investment opportunities, and firms in the high-tech sector are generally included here.
- Product longevity: Firms that sell products that last a long time and require support/service (e.g., cars) might see customers fleeing when the firms' financial situation gets precarious.
- Asset uniqueness: Firms with unique and specialized assets likely suffer more in a cash crunch because those assets cannot easily be sold to raise funds.
- Opacity: Opaque firms often find it harder and more expensive to raise funds than transparent firms, especially when they are financially distressed.
- Correlation with peers: Firms whose operations are correlated with their peers are likely to suffer more in a downturn, because many firms struggle at the same time, making it especially difficult to sell assets and raise funds.

These factors are important as firms consider the need to manage risk. If a firm does not exhibit any of the characteristics that make cash shortages costly, there is less need to curtail risk. You can think of the expected costs of running out of cash as the following: the probability of running out of cash × cost of running out of cash. If either the probability or cost is close to zero, we need not worry.

2.9   The need to project the future cash distribution

The next chapter focuses on estimating the distribution of future cash level. This, in turn, provides information about the likelihood of encountering ripple effects given the firm's current trajectory. But why should we engage in this exercise? Can't we just deal with the bad situation when/if it arises?

It is useful to know if there is a possible cash shortage looming on the horizon, because it is generally easier and more cost efficient to remedy the situation *before* encountering a cash shortage than when you actually have run out of cash. First, there are actions that we can take now to change the firm's trajectory but require some time to work, including reducing dividends and curbing growth. Second, there are actions that work to immediately raise the cash level but are cheaper and/or more attainable when the firm still has a solid cash position. For example, it is cheaper to raise cash from outside investors and banks when you already have cash. In fact, it might be impossible for a cash-strapped firm to find someone willing to extend it a loan. And any asset sales are likely to yield a higher price if the firm is financially sound than if it is weak and desperate.

3

Predicting and Simulating Liquidity

3.1 Predicting cash levels

The previous chapter emphasized the virtue of predicting cash positions, including the probability of cash shortages. To predict future cash levels, we will create pro forma statements. In particular, we want to forecast future balance sheets, where we observe the cash balance. But to do that, we also need to forecast future income statements, because the retained earnings from the income statement feed into the balance sheet.

We will loosely use the following four-step procedure:

i. Examine historical data.
ii. Forecast sales based on historical data, investment plans, and other information.
iii. Estimate other financial statement items, primarily by extrapolating the historical fractions of sales. A possible exception is property, plant, and equipment (PP&E), which follows from planned investments and depreciation. In fact, investments in PP&E facilitate sales growth. But regardless of whether you think of PP&E affecting sales growth or the other way around, PP&E and sales growth will be correlated over time.
iv. Estimate the *plug* to attain balance between assets and liabilities & equity. We will use cash balance as that plug.

Suppose that the tech company E-SPEN Inc. has the following past financial statements:

Income Statement	2018	2019	2020	2021
Net sales	$11,190	$13,764	$16,104	$20,613
Cost of goods sold	$9,400	$11,699	$13,688	$17,727

Applied Corporate Risk and Liquidity Management. Erik Lie, Oxford University Press. © Oxford University Press 2023.
DOI: 10.1093/oso/9780197664995.003.0003

Gross profit	$1,790	$2,065	$2,416	$2,886
Administrative expenses	$1,019	$1,239	$1,610	$2,267
Interest expenses	$100	$103	$110	$90
Income before tax	$671	$723	$696	$529
Tax (45%)	$302	$325	$313	$238
Earnings after tax	$369	$398	$383	$291
Dividends	$185	$199	$191	$145

Balance Sheet	2018	2019	2020	2021
Cash and securities	$671	$551	$643	$411
Accounts receivable	$1,343	$1,789	$2,094	$2,886
Inventory	$1,119	$1,376	$1,932	$2,267
Prepaid expenses	$14	$12	$15	$18
Total current assets	$3,147	$3,728	$4,684	$5,582
Net fixed assets	$128	$124	$295	$287
Total assets	$3,275	$3,852	$4,979	$5,869
Bank loan	$50	$50	$50	$50
Accounts payable	$1,007	$1,443	$2,426	$3,212
Current portion long-term debt	$60	$50	$50	$100
Accrued wages	$5	$7	$10	$18
Total current liabilities	$1,122	$1,550	$2,536	$3,380
Long-term debt	$960	$910	$860	$760
Common stock	$150	$150	$150	$150
Retained earnings	$1,043	$1,242	$1,433	$1,579
Total liabilities and equity	$3,275	$3,852	$4,979	$5,869

Based on these financial statements, I have calculated the following:

	2018	2019	2020	2021
Annual sales increase		23.0%	17.0%	28.0%
Percent of sales:				
COGS	84.0%	85.0%	85.0%	86.0%
Administrative expenses	9.1%	9.0%	10.0%	11.0%
Cash and securities	6.0%	4.0%	4.0%	2.0%

	2018	2019	2020	2021
A/R	12.0%	13.0%	13.0%	14.0%
Inventory	10.0%	10.0%	12.0%	11.0%
A/P	9.0%	10.5%	15.1%	15.6%
Dividend ratio	50.0%	50.0%	50.0%	50.0%

Let us now estimate the cash balance for 2022. To do so, I assumed that sales would grow by 22%, just a little below the average growth rate for the last few years. Other assumptions are given below, and they generally follow from historical ratios.

Income Statement

Net sales	$25,148	Growth of 22%
Cost of goods sold	$21,376	85% of sales
Gross profit	$3,772	
Administrative expenses	$2,515	10% of sales
Interest expenses	$80	About 10% of debt
Income before tax	$1,177	
Tax (45%)	$530	
Earnings after tax	$648	
Dividends	$324	50% of earnings

Balance Sheet

Cash and securities	$30	Plug
Accounts receivable	$3,521	14% of sales
Inventory	$2,515	10 of sales
Prepaid expenses	$20	
Total current assets	$6,085	
Net fixed assets	$320	According to investment plan
Total assets	$6,405	
Bank loan	$50	
Accounts payable	$3,521	14% of sales
Current portion long-term debt	$100	According to loan contract
Accrued wages	$22	Rough estimate
Total current liabilities	$3,693	
Long-term debt	$660	According to loan contract
Common stock	$150	
Retained earnings	$1,902	Beg. ret. earnings plus current year's ret. earnings
Total liabilities and equity	$6,405	

When we solve for the cash level, we see that it is $30. Of course, this is just a point estimate for next year's cash level, and there is a lot of uncertainty around our estimate. In fact, it is quite likely that it will be negative. To get more information about possible cash levels next year, we will resort to simulations.

3.2 Simulations

Many aspects of financial analysis focus on averages. For example, to estimate the value of a project, it is common to discount *expected* cash flow, which represents the *average* of possible cash flow outcomes. However, the average is often an insufficient statistic, especially when gauging liquidity risk, and we might want to know more about the distribution of possible outcomes. If you are about to cross a river on foot, as in Figure 3.1, wouldn't you want to know the maximum depth, and not just the average?

To gain further insight into the distribution of outcomes, it is common to estimate worst-case and best-case scenarios based on combinations of assumptions that are either bad or good for our outcome. However, it is unclear what the probabilities of those scenarios are. Furthermore, these additional scenarios still do not give a very complete picture of the full distribution. Figure 3.2 illustrates this for a company's future earnings. While the various scenarios seem to correspond to the underlying earnings distribution, the scenario analysis fails to indicate what the probabilities of the three scenarios are and whether even worse or better scenarios could occur.

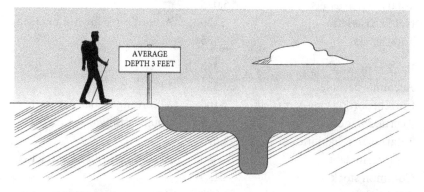

Figure 3.1 River crossing

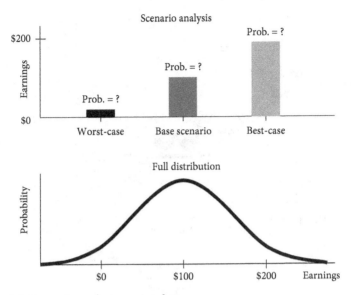

Figure 3.2 Scenario analysis vs. simulation

Simulations (also called Monte Carlo simulations, named after the *Monte Carlo Casino* in Monaco) are very useful for gauging the effect of multiple uncertain variables on some output variable, for example, the value of a portfolio at the end of the year.

The input variables are generally assigned a distribution of values, and they can also be allowed to correlate with each other. A computer model then makes use of the input variables along with other assumptions to simulate an array of possible outcomes for the predetermined output variable, which can be summarized in a histogram that illustrates the full distribution of outcomes. Figure 3.3 illustrates this process.

3.3 Simulations with Crystal Ball

It is possible to run simulations in Excel via a combination of the random number generator and tables. But simulations in Excel are greatly facilitated by Crystal Ball, which is an add-on to Excel. Thus, I use Crystal Ball here.

Once you have installed Crystal Ball, you get a separate menu tab in Excel. The most important commands in Crystal Ball menu are given in Figure 3.4, and I will refer to these later.

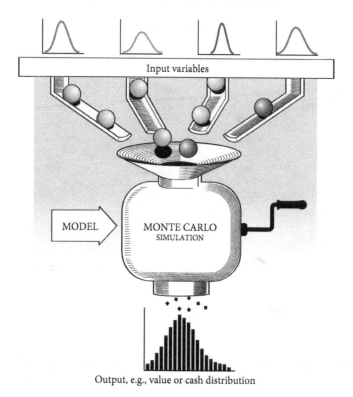

Figure 3.3 Monte Carlo simulation

Figure 3.4 Common Crystal Ball commands

Let us start with a simple example. You have invested $100,000 in a US stock index. Based on historical data and current economic variables (including prevailing interest rates), you estimate that the expected annual return on the index is 8% and the standard deviation of returns is 25%. Thus, on a monthly basis, the expected return is 0.643% ($1.00643^{12}-1 = 8\%$) and the standard deviation is 7.217% ($7.217\% \times \sqrt{12} = 25\%$). These values are given in cells D3 and E3, respectively, of my spreadsheet depicted in Figure 3.5.

As a first task, we want to simulate possible portfolio values after one month. The two values that determine the portfolio value after one month are the initial investment (which is fixed at $100,000) and the uncertain

◢	A	B	C	D	E	F	G	H
1		Annual		Monthly			Month	US index
2		Mean	Std dev	Mean	Std dev		1	-12.39%
3	US index	8%	25%	0.643%	7.217%			
4								
5	Investment	100,000						
6								
7	*Sim. end values*	Only US						
8	After one month	87,610						

Figure 3.5 Spreadsheet with investment value after one month

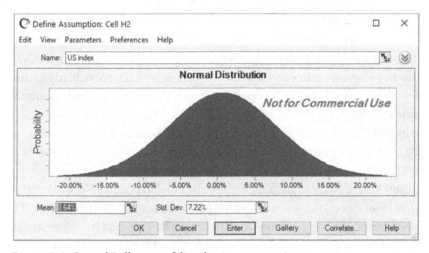

Figure 3.6 Crystal Ball input of distribution assumptions

return. In my spreadsheet, I have stored the investment value in cell B8, while the return for the next month is in cell H2. Because the return is uncertain, cell H2 contains information about possible outcomes. In particular, I first clicked on the cell and selected *Define Assumption* from the menu, which opened the box in Figure 3.6. I chose a normal distribution for the possible return outcomes for the next month.[1] For the mean, I referred to cell D3, though what you see is the actual value of 0.64%, and you could have entered this value directly. For the standard deviation, I referred to cell E3. Once this

---

[1] I think it is reasonable to use a normal distribution for short return periods, such as daily returns. But as the period gets longer, the return distribution turns lognormal, which we will see later. Thus, one could argue that I should have used a lognormal distribution for the monthly returns.

Figure 3.7 Crystal Ball input of forecast

is completed, the cell automatically turns bright green. This reminds us that this cell essentially contains a distribution of values.

The value of the portfolio is given in cell B8, and it is calculated as B5 × (1 + H2). This is the output variable of interest. Thus, I clicked cell B8 and selected *Define Forecast* from the menu, which opened the box in Figure 3.7. This also allowed me to name the output variable, which is particularly useful if we have several output variables (we will indeed introduce more output variables shortly). I named the output variable "After one month; only US" to indicate that this is the value after one month if our entire investment is in the US index. Upon completion, the cell automatically turns turquoise as a reminder that the cell contains an output variable.

Now we are ready to simulate some data. I like to start with one step/trial to make sure everything is working properly. You can run one simulation at a time by using the *Step* function from the menu. That is what I have done in the spreadsheet snapshot in Figure 3.5. The simulated return for the first month is −12.39%, and the resulting portfolio value after one month is $87,610.

Then I proceeded with the large-scale simulation. In the menu, I entered "1000000" for the number of trials and pressed *Start*. The box in Figure 3.8 opened. (I selected *Split View* from the *View* menu to see the summary statistics next to the distribution.) The mean value is given as 100,637, meaning that the portfolio value is expected to be $100,637 at the end of one month. With the mean return of 0.643%, the more accurate answer is $100,643, but the simulation results might be a little off. To improve accuracy, it would be possible to increase the number of trials. (Indeed, when I ran the simulation again using two million trials, I got a mean value of 100,644 instead, but that is not shown here.) The standard deviation from the simulation was 7,214, or 7.214% when scaled by the investment value of $100,000. This roughly corresponds to the standard deviation that we entered for the return of 7.217%. (We converge to 7.217% as we use even more trials.)

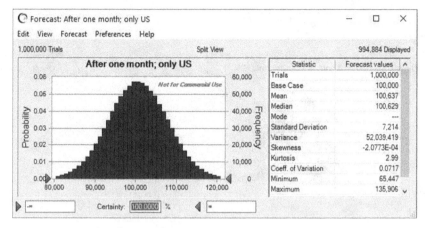

Figure 3.8 Simulated value after one month

	A	B	C	D	E	F	G	H	I
1		Annual		Monthly			Month	US index	Non-US ind.
2		Mean	Std dev	Mean	Std dev		1	4.46%	13.93%
3	US index	8%	25%	0.643%	7.217%		2	-0.29%	-5.89%
4	Non-US index	10%	30%	0.797%	8.660%		3	4.47%	-7.70%
5							4	17.69%	9.29%
6	Correlation	50%					5	-1.36%	-11.55%
7							6	15.94%	9.51%
8	Investment	100,000					7	-1.11%	17.39%
9							8	-1.38%	-2.44%
10	Sim. end values	Only US	Non-US	Both			9	-4.48%	3.85%
11	After one month	104,458	113,929	109,194			10	3.22%	7.24%
12	After 12 months	135,307	125,526	130,417			11	-8.82%	-6.52%
13							12	5.38%	0.50%
14							Total	35.31%	25.53%

Figure 3.9 Spreadsheet with investment value after 12 months

Now we will extend the simulation to include the whole year. That is, we will simulate the returns for each of 12 months and estimate the portfolio value at the end of the year based on the returns for the 12 months. Figure 3.9 shows the spreadsheet. Cells H2–H13 contain the returns for each of the 12 months.[2] Cell H14 cumulates the returns, that is, $(1 + \text{return}_1) \times (1 + \text{return}_2) \times \ldots \times (1 + \text{return}_{12}) - 1$. The value at the end of the year is given in cell B12, and it is

[2] I simply copied the content from cell H2 to cells H3–H13. Note that to copy the entire distribution information, you must use the copy and paste commands from the Crystal Ball menu. The regular copy and paste commands only copy the value and the format, including the color, which might fool you into thinking that both cells contain Crystal Ball assumptions.

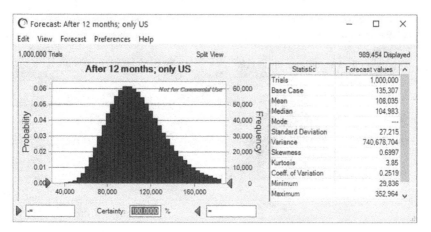

Figure 3.10 Simulated value after one year

calculated as B8 × (1 + H14). After defining cell B12 as another output variable using the *Define Forecast* command and naming it "After 12 months; only US," it also turned turquoise.

When I ran another simulation based on one million trials, I got the results in Figure 3.10. The mean is now 108,035 and the standard deviation is 27,215. We also see that the distribution is asymmetric, which is clear from just looking at the distribution or comparing the mean to the median (the mean differs from the median for an asymmetric distribution). The intuition is that, over time, there is a limit to how much money we can lose (i.e., our entire investment of $100,000), but there is essentially no limit to how much we can gain. Thus, the earlier normal distribution becomes lognormal. In short, the return distribution is approximately normal for short periods, such as days, but over longer periods, such as years, the return distribution is approximately lognormal.

As a last step to the simulation exercise, I also introduced an alternative investment. This is a non-US index with an expected annual return of 10% and a standard deviation of 30%. Furthermore, the correlation between the US index and the non-US index is 50%. Cells I2–I13 contain the returns for the non-US index for each of the next 12 months. I entered the information like I did for the US index, but I naturally used the higher return and standard deviation estimates for the non-US index. In addition, I entered the correlation information by clicking the *Correlate* button inside the *Define Assumption* box.[3]

---

[3] If we have multiple securities/indices in our portfolio, it is possible to insert the whole correlation matrix into Crystal Ball in one step.

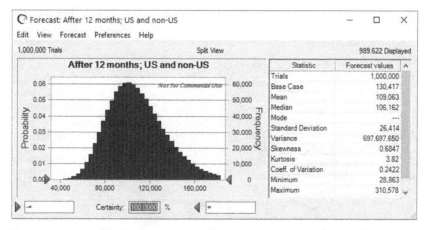

Figure 3.11 Simulated value after one year with international diversification

I assumed that I invested $50,000 in the US index and $50,000 in the non-US index, and then estimated the value at the end of one year in cell D12. I further used *Define Forecast* to select D12 as another output variable that I named "After 12 months; US and non-US."

Another simulation with one million trials yielded the results in Figure 3.11. The mean is now 109,063, meaning that the expected portfolio value after one year is $109,063. The standard deviation is $26,414. Comparing these simulation results to the results when investing only in the US index, we see that the mean is higher while the standard deviation is *lower*. Are you surprised? The lower standard deviation happened despite the higher standard deviation for the non-US index, and it serves as an illustration of portfolio theory at work when securities are imperfectly correlated.

3.4 Value at Risk (VaR) and the tails of the distribution

As an investor or portfolio manager, you might also ask yourself what the worst-case scenario is over the next year. That is, if you invest in both the US and non-US indices, how much of that investment is "at risk"? Let us try to define "at risk" a little better. Suppose that we agree that it is very unlikely that the value will fall in the 5% tail of the distribution. (We can at least agree that it is 95% certain that the value will *not* fall in the 5% tail.) So let us set the upper value of the 5% tail as the "minimum" value of the investment at the

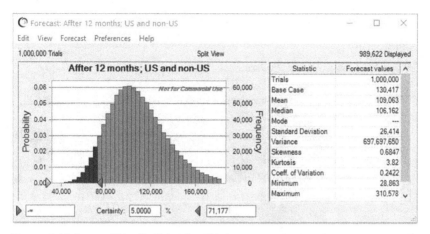

Figure 3.12 Lower 5% tail of simulated value

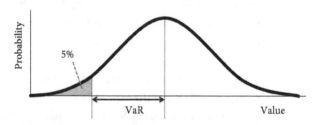

Figure 3.13 Typical illustration of VaR

end of relevant period. Then the "maximum" that we can lose equals the difference between the current value and the upper value of the 5% tail.

Consider the distribution of our portfolio value at the end of the year again. I have marked the lower 5% tail in Figure 3.12. The upper value of the 5% tail is $71,177. Given that the current investment value is $100,000, we could say that the "maximum" loss (or at least the maximum reasonable loss) is $100,000−$71,177 = $28,823. We call this *Value at Risk*, or *VaR* for short. *VaR* is a measure of risk based on a probability distribution of possible outcomes during a specified period, and it gives an indication of the maximum reasonable loss in value. The loss is generally defined by the 5% lower tail, as in the example above.

Figure 3.13 is the typical illustration of *VaR* as the difference between the average of the distribution and the upper value of the 5% tail.

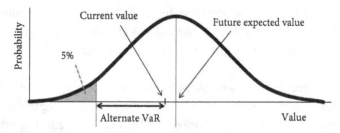

Figure 3.14 Alternative illustration of VaR

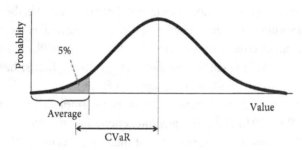

Figure 3.15 Illustration of CVaR

A caveat is that in my example I estimated *VaR* as the difference between the *current value* of the investment and the upper value of the 5% tail, because that makes conceptually more sense to me as the loss the portfolio could suffer. Figure 3.14 illustrates my alternate *VaR*.

VaR is a useful and widely used tool because of its relatively easy calculation, clear interpretation, and important implication for portfolio managers. But, as with all simulation output, *VaR* critically depends on our assumptions about return distributions and correlations. Indeed, some have argued that the downfall of the hedge fund *Long Term Capital Management* before the turn of the century was due to underestimation of the correlations across markets. (Who could have predicted that the Southeast Asian currency crisis would spread and Russia would default on its bonds at the same time?)

Another useful measure is *Conditional Value at Risk* (*CVaR*), which is the difference between the current value and the average of the values in the lower tail and is illustrated in Figure 3.15. In other words, it answers this question: "If things get really bad, what value can we expect to lose?"

Finally, I should note that one can simply replace the value in *VaR* with, for example, cash flow or cash to get *Cash Flow at Risk* (*CFaR*) or *Cash at Risk*

(*CaR*), respectively (ok, so the latter term, *CaR*, is not used anywhere else than here). That brings us back to our analysis of cash levels.

Before we proceed, a couple of warnings are in order:

- We commonly report some statistics associated with the tail of the distribution, such as the lower 5% value. But what about also reporting the minimum or maximum values of the distribution? I recommend against reporting, or at least focusing on, the minimum or maximum values of the distribution for two reasons. First, in a simulation of, say 100,000 trials, the minimum and maximum values are very unlikely, occurring with a probability of only 0.001% each. Second, unlike the lower and higher 5% values, the minimum and maximum values are a function of the number of trials in the simulation. For example, the minimum value is likely to be much smaller in a simulation of one million trials than in a simulation of 1,000 trials. That is, the minimum value decreases as we increase the number of trials.
- Simulations give very precise answers. For example, we might estimate that VaR is $104,741.12. But *precision often conceals inaccuracy*; just because the answer is precise does not mean it is accurate. The accuracy also depends on how reasonable the assumptions we make for the simulation are. Thus, I prefer to round the output from simulations so that no one is deceived into thinking that it is highly accurate. For example, I might round the VaR above to $105,000, or perhaps even $100,000.

3.5 Simulated cash levels

Now that we understand Crystal Ball, let us forecast the cash distribution. Our focus is on determining the probability that there is a cash shortfall, as illustrated in Figure 3.16. Traditional risk measures, such as standard

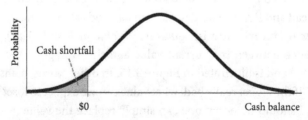

Figure 3.16 Cash shortfall

	A	B	C	D	E	F	G
1		2022	2023E				
2							
3	Sales	$200,000	$220,000	10%	10%	4%	Growth
4	Variable costs	$160,000	$176,000	80%	80%	3%	Fraction of sales
5	Fixed costs	$20,000	$20,000	0%	0%	2%	Growth
6	Interest expense	$3,000	$3,000				
7	Profit	$17,000	$21,000				
8	Tax (21%)	$3,570	$4,410				
9	Net profit	$13,430	$16,590				
10							
11							
12	Cash	$10,000	$15,590				Plug
13	Non-cash CA	$70,000	$77,000	35%	35%	3%	Fraction of sales
14	PP&E	$120,000	$130,000				Investment plan
15	Total assets	$200,000	$222,590				
16							
17	CL	$60,000	$66,000	30%	30%	3%	Fraction of sales
18	LT debt	$50,000	$50,000				
19	Equity	$90,000	$106,590				
20		$200,000	$222,590				

Figure 3.17 Spreadsheet with pro forma statements

deviation, are of less interest to the extent that we believe the greatest costs are incurred for negative cash balances.

Figure 3.17 shows a spreadsheet with a simplified income statement and balance sheet for 2022 and corresponding pro forma statements for 2023. Row E provides assumptions on the growth in sales and fixed costs as well as the fraction of variable costs, non-cash current assets, and current liabilities of sales. Row F provides the standard deviations for the same variables. Row D contains the input variables for the simulation, which is why the cells are green. For example, cell D3 contains a normal distribution with a mean of 10% (from cell E3) and standard deviation of 4% (from cell F3), and it affects cell C3, which includes the formula B3 × (1 + D3).

Figure 3.18 shows the formulas behind the numbers in the spreadsheet. It is particularly noteworthy to see how I avoided circularity (which Excel would warn you about, but that warning tends to confuse people) and ensured balance in the balance sheet. The total assets are simply calculated as the sum of all individual asset items. But then cash cannot be estimated as total assets less non-cash asset items because that would cause circularity and would fail to ensure balance in the balance sheet. Rather, cash is estimated as total liabilities and equity less non-cash items. This avoids circularity and

	A	B	C	D	E	F	G
1		2022	2023E				
2							
3	Sales	200000	=B3*(1+D3)	0.1	0.1	0.04	Growth
4	Variable costs	160000	=D4*C3	0.8	0.8	0.03	Fraction of sales
5	Fixed costs	20000	=B5*(1+D5)	0	0	0.02	Growth
6	Interest expense	3000	3000				
7	Profit	=B3-B4-B5-B6	=C3-C4-C5-C6				
8	Tax (21%)	=0.21*B7	=0.21*C7				
9	Net profit	=B7-B8	=C7-C8				
10							
11							
12	Cash	10000	=C20-C14-C13				Plug
13	Non-cash CA	70000	=D13*C3	0.35	0.35	0.03	Fraction of sales
14	PP&E	120000	130000				Investment plan
15	Total assets	=B12+B13+B14	=C12+C13+C14				
16							
17	CL	60000	=D17*C3	0.3	0.3	0.03	Fraction of sales
18	LT debt	50000	50000				
19	Equity	90000	=B19+C9				
20		=B17+B18+B19	=C17+C18+C19				

Figure 3.18 Underlying formulas in spreadsheet

ensures balance in the balance sheet. (An alternative approach would be to set total assets equal to total liabilities and equity, and then estimate cash as total assets less non-cash asset items.)

Figure 3.19 shows one random trial after selecting *Step* from the Crystal Ball menu. In this trial, the cash is only $797, compared to $15,590 in the base scenario. Given that our setup seems to work for one trial, we are ready to launch more trials to see the entire cash distribution.

Figure 3.20 shows the output from the simulation of one million trials. We are particularly interested in cash shortages because they likely induce ripple effects. Thus, I inserted the value of 0 in the lower right of the box, such that the value of 7.2812% appears as the probability that the cash level is below $0. In short, the cash analysis shows that the expected cash level for 2023 is above $10,000, and the probability that we face a cash shortage is roughly 7%. I would conclude that the firm carries a reasonably safe cash level (and certainly not excessive), and it is unlikely, but still very possible, that the firm will experience ripple effects in the next year from tight liquidity. In other words, the firm probably has sufficient cash to make the necessary investments and will not have to resort to expensive fundraising. But you could very well

	A	B	C	D	E	F	G
1		2022	2023E				
2							
3	Sales	$200,000	$202,675	1%	10%	4%	Growth
4	Variable costs	$160,000	$160,165	79%	80%	3%	Fraction of sales
5	Fixed costs	$20,000	$20,409	2%	0%	2%	Growth
6	Interest expense	$3,000	$3,000				
7	Profit	$17,000	$19,101				
8	Tax (21%)	$3,570	$4,011				
9	Net profit	$13,430	$15,090				
10							
11							
12	Cash	$10,000	$797				Plug
13	Non-cash CA	$70,000	$77,983	38%	35%	3%	Fraction of sales
14	PP&E	$120,000	$130,000				Investment plan
15	Total assets	$200,000	$208,780				
16							
17	CL	$60,000	$53,689	26%	30%	3%	Fraction of sales
18	LT debt	$50,000	$50,000				
19	Equity	$90,000	$105,090				
20		$200,000	$208,780				

Figure 3.19 Spreadsheet with random trial values

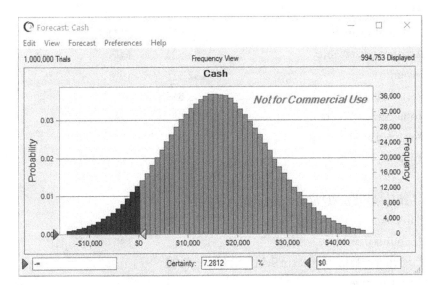

Figure 3.20 Simulated cash value

argue that another $10,000 in cash is warranted here to be on the safe side, especially if the cost of a shortfall is significant.

Let us return to the earlier example of E-SPEN Inc. The pro forma statements are repeated below, but now I have defined the assumptions as

Crystal Ball input variables, where the means are the same as I used as the base assumptions earlier, and the standard deviations are given to the right of the respective green input cells.

Income Statement

Net sales	$25,148	22%	5%
Cost of goods sold	$21,376	85%	1%
Gross Profit	$3,772		
Administrative expenses	$2,515	10%	1%
Interest expenses	$80		
Income before tax	$1,177		
Tax (45%)	$530		
Earnings after tax	$648		
Dividends	$324		

Balance Sheet

ASSETS:

Cash and securities	$30	PLUG	
Accounts receivable	$3,521	14%	1%
Inventory	$2,515	10%	1%
Prepaid expenses	$20		
Total current assets	$6,085		
Net fixed assets	$320		
Total	$6,405		

LIABILITIES AND EQUITY:

Bank loan	$50		
Accounts payable	$3,521	14%	1%
Current portion long-term debt	$100		
Accrued wages	$22		
Total current liabilities	$3,693		
Long-term debt	$660		
Common stock	$150		
Retained earnings	$1,902		
Total	$6,405		

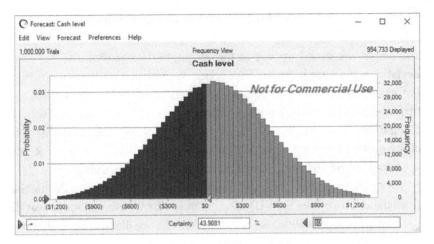

Figure 3.21 Simulated cash value for E-SPEN

Figure 3.21 provides the simulation output for 1,000,000 trials. The cash level is dangerously low. While the firm is expected to have some cash at the end of the year, there is a 44% probability that the firm will have run out of cash. Furthermore, it appears that it would take another $500–1,000 to get on safe ground. It is very useful to know this now because we can take action to avoid possible future ripple effects. For example, we could cut the dividends. Or we could raise some external capital while the firm still looks financially solid (recall that the current cash balance is more than $400). Or we might slow down the rapid growth that requires so much capital, for example, by reducing capital investments or raising prices. The next section on risk management explores how we can reduce the uncertainty in the cash level.

Our simulations should capture the full range of scenarios. Thus, there is no need to run an additional set of, for example, "worst-case scenarios." This might be obvious. But I am pointing it out because I occasionally observe this misconception.

We can easily extend the simulation to more years. But if we do so, we need to draw a new set of trials for each of those years even if the distributions are assumed to be constant. For example, revenues might be expected to increase by 10% in each of the next three years, with a standard deviation of 5%. Yet the growth for each year must be drawn independently. We will see this in a later example.

3.6 Standard deviation assumptions

You might ask how I arrived at the assumptions regarding the standard deviations. If we are lucky, we have access to some market-based estimates. For example, as a measure for the future standard deviation of stock return, it is possible to back out the volatility from option premiums (simply Google "implied volatility calculator" for a framework to do this). The volatility index VIX—also referred to as the fear index—is an example of this approach for the S&P 500 index. Figure 3.22 shows historical values of VIX, which hover around 15–20% in normal times and peaked at 80% during the financial crisis and the COVID-19 pandemic when there was much fear in the market. The volatilities for individual stocks are likely to be higher because they also contain idiosyncratic uncertainty.

But chances are that we are not so lucky to have market-based estimates. In that case, we face a much greater challenge in estimating standard deviations.

When making standard deviation assumptions, I find it useful to consider what standard deviations imply. For a normal distribution, as in Figure 3.23, it is about 68% certain that the observations will fall within one standard deviation of the mean and 95% certain that the observations will fall within two standard deviations of the mean. For example, if I set the expected sales growth to be 10% with a standard deviation of 4%, I am implicitly saying that I am 95% confident that the sales growth will be between $10\% - 2 \times 4\% = 2\%$ and $10\% + 2 \times 4\% = 18\%$. In other words, the 95% confidence interval is [2%, 18%]. If I think this is too narrow or wide, I adjust the standard deviation accordingly. This is undoubtedly quite subjective.

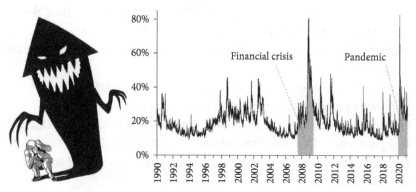

Figure 3.22 Volatility index (a.k.a. fear index)

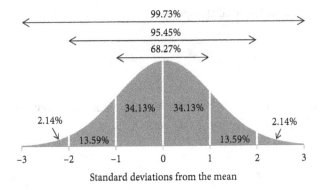

Figure 3.23 Normal distribution

A warning is in order when relying on subjective confidence intervals. People, and especially corporate executives, tend to be overly confident. Strong evidence of overconfidence comes from studies in which participants are asked to specify confidence intervals of specific quantities. In the absence of overconfidence, their X% confidence intervals would include the correct answer X% of the time. For example, I have occasionally asked students to individually write down the 95% confidence interval for the population of a country, say Norway (which incidentally has a population of about five million). When I then ask the students to raise their hands if their confidence interval contained the actual population of five million, I should see 95% of the students raising their hands. However, I rarely see more than half of the hands raised, not because the students are too shy to raise their hands, but simply because too many were overly confident in their ability to gauge the population size.

With a long historical time series, you can estimate historical standard deviations. However, historical standard deviations are not quite the same as future standard deviations, both because there might be changes in the business environment (e.g., a jump in political risk from an upcoming election) and because variations over time might be expected. Let us elaborate on the latter point.

The change in a given variable (e.g., sales) from one period to the next can be written as:

Total change = Expected change + Unexpected change

and the variance of the total change is:

$$\sigma_\Delta^2 = \sigma_{\Delta Expected}^2 + \sigma_{\Delta Unexpected}^2 + 2\rho\sigma_{\Delta Expected}\sigma_{\Delta Unexpected}$$

It is further reasonable to believe that the correlation between expected and unexpected changes, ρ, is zero, so we get:

$$\sigma_\Delta^2 = \sigma_{\Delta Expected}^2 + \sigma_{\Delta Unexpected}^2 \Rightarrow \sigma_{\Delta Unexpected}^2 = \sigma_\Delta^2 - \sigma_{\Delta Expected}^2$$

The standard deviation we need for the simulation should capture the *uncertainty* of the distribution, and, thus, refers to the unexpected change. That is, we would like to have an estimate of $\sigma_{\Delta Unexpected}$. But it might be tricky to disentangle historical changes into expected and unexpected components. If we estimate standard deviation of total changes, the equation above suggests that our estimate is biased upward. Thus, we can view our estimated standard deviation as a ceiling for what we seek.

In general, the magnitude of the upward bias in using historical standard deviations as estimates of future uncertainty depends on the data. For daily stock return data, the bias is likely to be minor, because the expected stock return on a single day is small (typically less than 0.1%) and hardly changes over time (suggesting a low standard deviation), whereas the actual daily stock returns vary substantially (with perhaps half of the absolute daily returns exceeding 1%). Conversely, for annual sales or earnings data, the bias can be substantial.

Let me illustrate with a couple of examples. Consider Figure 3.24, which depicts historical sales. The average historical growth rate is 6.3%, and the standard deviation of growth is 14.9%. Based on an expected future growth of 5% and a standard deviation of 14.9%, I have drawn the 95% confidence interval for next year's sales. If past changes were largely unexpected, this confidence interval is reasonable.

Now consider the sales in Figure 3.25. The average historical growth rate is 19.4%, and the standard deviation of growth is 19.1%. While the standard deviation is relatively high, we see that the sales growth was quite predictable, with a rapid growth initially that tapers off gradually over time. Thus, one can argue that the standard deviation yields a deceptive picture of the uncertainty of the growth. The two confidence intervals for

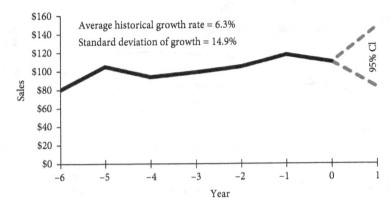

Figure 3.24 Historical sales

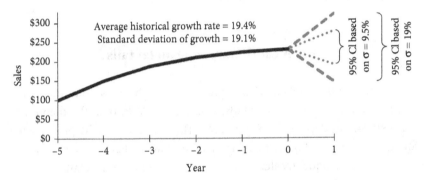

Figure 3.25 Historical sales with predictable growth rate

next year's sales illustrate this further. The 95% confidence interval based on the historical standard deviation of growth of 19.1% seems much too wide. In my opinion, the 95% confidence interval based on a more reasonable standard deviation of 9.5% seems more reasonable. Perhaps it should even be narrower.

Last, consider the sales in Figure 3.26. The year-to-year changes are modest, except for the dramatic increase from year −4 to −3. But the dots (which indicate the expected sales levels as of the prior year) show that the dramatic increase from year −4 to −3 was expected, perhaps because a new product was introduced to the market in year −3. If we base the confidence interval on the realized standard deviation of growth of 26%, the confidence interval seems much too wide. But if we instead base the confidence interval

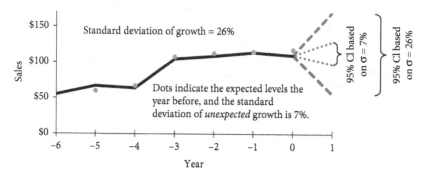

Figure 3.26 Historical sales with an anticipated jump

on the standard deviation of the *unexpected* growth rate of 7%, the confidence interval seems far more reasonable.

3.7 A cautionary note on fat tails

We often assume normal and lognormal distributions. But many actual distributions have heavier tails, so-called *fat tails*, than the theoretical distributions, as depicted in Figure 3.27. This seems especially pronounced for stock returns and other financial data. As Eugene Fama, Nobel Laureate in Economics, eloquently stated in an interview: "Life has a fat tail."

For illustration, consider a distribution with normal tails. Individual heights are often assumed to be normally distributed. Adult male heights are, on average, 70 inches with a standard deviation of 4 inches. In the United States, the tallest man is 92 inches, which is $(92–70)/4 = 5.5$

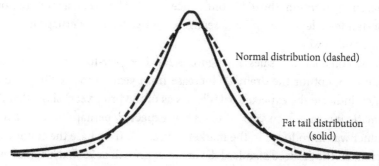

Figure 3.27 Fat tail distribution

standard deviations from the mean. If the heights are truly normally distributed, such a height should statistically occur in one of 50 million men. Given a population of about 120 million men in the United States, this seems reasonable.

In contrast, let us consider household income. Good data on household income is hard to obtain, but roughly 95% of US households have an income between $5,000 and $250,000, and the distribution is clearly skewed. If household income is lognormally distributed, then *ln* household income is normally distributed. Based on the normal distribution, 95% of observations should be between *ln* 5000 = 8.5 and *ln* 250,000 = 12.4, and the mean should be about (8.5+12.4)/2 = 10.45 and the standard deviation should be (12.4–8.5)/4 ≈ 1. Bill Gates reportedly has an income above $10,000,000,000 (presumably depending heavily on his portfolio performance), and *ln* 10,000,000,000 = 20.7, which is about (20.7–10.45)/1 ≈ 10 standard deviations away from the mean. Even in a solar system of one billion planets just like Earth, we would be unlikely to find such an outlier on any of the planets if household income truly were lognormally distributed. Outliers like Bill Gates and many others suggest that the income distribution has a fat tail.

As another example of fat tails, consider the stock returns of Casey's General Stores, Inc. I downloaded daily adjusted price data from finance. yahoo.com (which are adjusted for dividends and splits) from 2000 through 2020 and calculated daily returns. Based on the daily returns, I estimated the average return to be 0.08% and the standard deviation to be 2.11%. Figure 3.28 shows the distribution of the daily returns along with a normal distribution with the same average and standard deviation. It is hard to see the fat tails here, but you know that they must be there for the standard

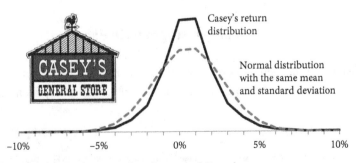

Figure 3.28 The stock return distribution of Casey's

deviations of the graphs to be the same (and the fat tails actually extend beyond the scale of the graph).

If the return distribution had been normal, roughly 95% of the daily returns should be within two standard deviations of the mean (i.e., from −4.15 to + 4.3%), which can be roughly verified from a quick glance at the normal distribution in the graph. But on February 28, 2002, the price dropped by 19%, and on December 4, 2008, it dropped by 20%. Furthermore, on March 10, 2009, the price increased by 27%, and on April 9, 2010, it increased by 24%. These returns are all more than eight standard deviations from the mean. The largest (27%) is almost 13 standard deviations away. If the returns were truly normally distributed, a return that is eight standard deviations away from the mean should statistically occur less than once in a *trillion years!*[4] Evidently, extreme outliers occur in the return data much more frequently than the normal distribution suggests.

It is common to ignore fat tails, which can have dire consequences. Leicester City FC won the 2015/16 Premier league in football (or "soccer" for the confused American reader), despite odds of 5,000 to 1 before the season. While some argue that this was the largest surprise in sports history, most sports history is not that long, perhaps just 100 years long. Was it truly the case that Leicester would statistically only win once in 5,000 years? Another example is the 2008 flood in Iowa City. The flood caused major damage to many major buildings at the University of Iowa campus. Presumably, this was highly unanticipated, or there wouldn't have been so many buildings in the floodplain. Generally, statistical models are developed to map 50-year floodplains, 100-year floodplains, etc. But fat tails seem to cause these so-called 50-year floods, etc., to occur more often than their names suggest. Consequently, buildings are erected in locations where they are quite likely to be severely damaged during their lives.

3.8 Making histograms in Excel

While Crystal Ball generates histograms, they come with constraints. In this section, I first create overlaid histograms for our earlier example on returns

---

[4] You can play with these probabilities yourself using Excel's NORMSDIST(Z) function, which gives the cumulative probability given Z standard deviations from the mean.

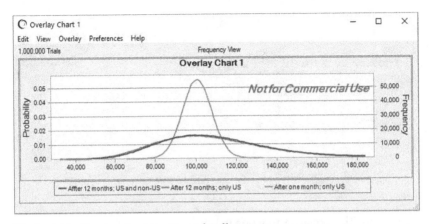

Figure 3.29 Overlay charts in Crystal Ball

for one month and a year using Crystal Ball. Then I do the same using basic Excel functions.

We already created histograms for the individual output variables (one month ahead using only the US index, one year ahead using only the US index, and one year ahead using both the US and non-US indices). Combining these histograms into overlay charts greatly facilitates comparison of the histograms.

From the Crystal Ball menu, select *Overlay Charts* from *View Charts* after running the simulation. Then select *New* and choose the distributions to be included in the overlay chart. (I chose the *Chart Type* under *Preferences* to be *Line* instead of the default of *Column*, because the latter makes it difficult to see all overlaid distributions.) Figure 3.29 displays the graph. Crystal Ball allows little flexibility in improving the appearance further.

Now, let us create a similar graph using the basic functions of Excel. First, download the Crystal Ball simulation values data by selecting *Extract Data* and then *Trial values*. Then we need to count the number of observations in predefined bins. This can be done quickly using the *Histogram* add-in feature in *Data Analysis*.[5] However, I prefer to rely on either frequency or count functions to make the histogram dynamic (meaning that I can interactively change the underlying data, bin sizes, etc.), and I can just slightly modify the spreadsheet when I need to make a new histogram. Figure 3.30 shows

---

[5] Excel even allows you to highlight the data and choose *Histogram* from its menu of charts to easily make a dynamic histogram. However, the formatting is limited. For example, while you can adjust bin widths, you are limited to making columns (and not a line) for one time series at a time.

Trial values	After one month; only US	After 12 months; only US	Affter 12 months; US and non-US			High bin value	Mid bin value	One month; US	One year; US	One year; US and non-US
1	$94,828	$120,631	$93,754	Min	$39,000	$39,000	Less	0	82	33
2	$89,254	$90,331	$96,628	Bin size	$2,000	$41,000	$40,000	0	79	46
3	$102,799	$113,142	$117,858			$43,000	$42,000	0	126	63
4	$99,752	$106,985	$98,352			$45,000	$44,000	0	252	120

Trial values	After one month; only US	After 12 months; only US	Affter 12 months; US and non-US			High bin value	Mid bin value	One month; US	One year; US	One year; US and non-US
1	94828.24!	120631.2!	93754.33!	Min	39000	=G2	Less	=FREQUENCY(B:B,$I:$I)	=FREQUENCY(C:C,$I:$I)	=FREQUENCY(D:D,$I:$I)
2	89254.06!	90330.57!	96627.87!	Bin size	2000	=I2+G$3	=AVERAGE(I2:I3)			
3	102798.7!	113141.6!	117858.0!			=I3+G$3	=AVERAGE(I3:I4)			
4	99752.47!	106985.4!	98351.77!			=I4+G$3	=AVERAGE(I4:I5)			
5	109246.3!	145162.6!	148765.8!			=I5+G$3	=AVERAGE(I5:I6)			

Figure 3.30 The frequency function in Excel

the frequency function in action. There are a few things worth noticing. First, I chose the minimum bin values and bin size in cells G2 and G3 so that I would get about 50–100 bins that would capture most of the values. Second, the frequency function spills over to the cells below, so it only needs to be inserted at the top of the rows (in cells K2, L2, and M2 in my example). Third, the bin values in column I (that the frequency function uses as input) represent the high value of a bin range. Because I like to use the mid-value of a bin range for the graph, I estimate the mid-value in column J.

Then I highlight the data in rows J–M and select *Line Chart*. After some further tailoring (e.g., making the lines smooth and removing the y-axis, which serves no purpose here), I get the graph in Figure 3.31.

It is also possible to shade some part of the distribution. Figure 3.32 shows the distribution for the one-year returns (US and non-US) again. I have also shaded the lower 5% of the distribution. To do that, I used two

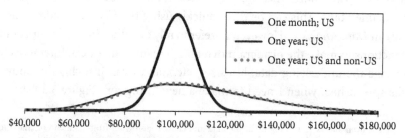

——	One month; US
——	One year; US
• • • •	One year; US and non-US

$40,000 $60,000 $80,000 $100,000 $120,000 $140,000 $160,000 $180,000

Figure 3.31 Distributions of investment values

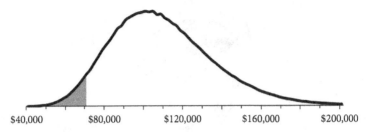

$40,000 $80,000 $120,000 $160,000 $200,000

Figure 3.32 Distribution with shaded lower 5% tail

data columns. The first data column contains the bin counts corresponding to the one-year returns (which I also used in the graph above). The second data column is the same as the first data column, except that the cells are blank for all bins above the ones that I want to be shaded. Thus, I end up with two overlapping distributions, except that the second only covers the lower part. To change the second distribution into a shaded area, I right-clicked the second data series, selected *Change Series Chart Type*, and chose *Area* chart type.

3.9 Goldman predicts the World Cup

Bloomberg ran the following headline on June 11, 2018: "Goldman Tips Brazil for World Cup After 1 Million Simulations." The article further stated that the investment bank Goldman Sachs "used 200,000 statistical models, sifted data on individual players and recent team performance and ran 1 million simulations of the tournament. As a result, it predicts that Brazil will lift the trophy on July 15."

This sounds impressive, right? I find the emphasis on the number of simulations to be particularly interesting, as it seems to suggest that one million simulations yield a much more accurate prediction than, say, 100,000 simulations. Of course, what determines the predictive power of a simulation model is not the number of trials (given that it is above a reasonable number), but rather the assumptions that go into the model, as Figure 3.33 humorously depicts.

Incidentally, several later articles made fun of the failure of Goldman's model to come even close to predicting the outcome of the World Cup. (If you do not know, France beat Croatia in the final.) But while the incorrect prediction might suggest that Goldman's model is "wrong," it might alternatively

Figure 3.33 Simulation model for the World Cup

be interpreted as evidence that even the best model has limited predictive power in the face of great uncertainty.

To be fair, Goldman's model did not actually predict that Brazil winning the trophy was the most likely outcome, as Bloomberg's article insinuated, but rather that Brazil, at close to 20%, had the highest probability of winning of the 32 participating nations. So even Goldman's model predicted that there was an 80% chance that Brazil would <u>not</u> win.

4

Risk Management Theory

4.1 Individual risk aversion

I find it easiest to start with a discussion on preferences for individuals. Individuals are generally presumed to be averse to risk, and this can be explained in a utility framework.

Suppose that individuals try to maximize expected utility, whether we derive utility from wealth, leisure time, experiences, friendships, or something else. Furthermore, suppose that the utility function is concave. That means that the first million dollars you accumulate provides more utility than the second, the first glass of water after a workout provides more utility than the second, the first week of vacation in Italy provides more utility than the second, one good friend provides more utility than the second, etc.

Figure 4.1 shows a concave utility function. Suppose that you have wealth of w_1, say $1 million, which you could bet to get either w_2, say $200,000, or w_3, say $1.8 million, with equal probabilities. Both the certain $1 million and the bet give an expected wealth of $1 million. However, while the certain $1 million gives an expected utility of u_1, the bet gives an expected utility of $(u_2 + u_3)/2$, which is less than u_1. Thus, individuals who maximize their utility prefer the safe path to the risky bet. That is, they are risk averse.

4.2 Corporate risk aversion and hedging

While individuals arguably maximize utility, corporations clearly do not, and cannot given that corporations do not have utility functions. Rather, the primary objective of corporations is to maximize the wealth of their owners, that is, shareholders. Some might argue that other stakeholders, such as employees, should also be considered as part of the objective function, while others would argue that considering stakeholders is completely

Applied Corporate Risk and Liquidity Management. Erik Lie, Oxford University Press. © Oxford University Press 2023.
DOI: 10.1093/oso/9780197664995.003.0004

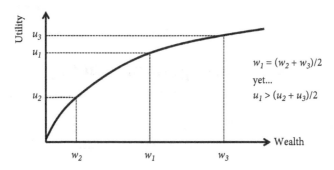

Figure 4.1 Concave utility function

consistent with maximizing shareholder value. One might also argue that corporate decisions are made by managers, who maximize their own utility. True. And we will get back to the potential diverging interests of managers and owners. For now, we will assume that the corporate objective is to maximize shareholders' wealth.

Given the corporate objective to maximize shareholder value, a relevant question is whether risk affects that value. If not, there is no need to engage in risk management.

Portfolio theory tells us that risk is positively related to security returns, and this is formalized in the CAPM (Capital Asset Pricing Model). The CAPM, in turn, is used to estimate the cost of capital, and with a higher cost of capital, the value falls. In that sense, firm risk adversely affects corporate value.

An important caveat is that the CAPM only considers *systematic* risk. In contrast, *firm-specific* risk is diversifiable and therefore not priced. Most of a firm's risk is firm-specific, such as the risk of a product failure or a machine breakdown. Other risk factors that firms frequently hedge, like commodity price risk, fall somewhere between systematic and firm-specific risk, in that they often affect various segments of the economy in different ways while the overall economy is relatively unaffected.

Let us then ask a more challenging question: Do firm-specific and commodity risk factors affect corporate value? And I am not asking whether, say, a decline in oil prices affects the value of oil firms—it obviously does. Rather I am asking whether greater volatility in oil prices affects the value of oil firms.

4.3 The benefit of corporate hedging: An example

Froot, Scharfstein, and Stein (1993) developed a framework for risk management that shows how risk affects corporate value. As Figure 4.2 shows, they base their framework on three premises:

1. The key to creating corporate value is making good investment decisions.
2. The key to making good investment decisions is to have available internal funds (because external funds are unavailable or too expensive).
3. External factors, such as commodity prices, affect internal funds.

We can all agree on the first and third of these premises. The second is more controversial. You might recognize that it is related to the earlier discussion on ripple effects. That is, if a firm runs short on cash, it might not be possible to replenish that cash (at least not without paying a cost), which is why the ripple effects surface. In this case, the ripple effect is that a cash-constrained firm invests suboptimally.

Let us consider an example. North Sea Oil AS will generate either $100, $200, or $300, depending on oil prices. It can spend the funds on exploration activities. Investments of $100, $200, and 300 yield expected NPVs of $30, $40, and $20, respectively, meaning that $200 is the optimal investment level. Figure 4.3 summarizes these assumptions.

Figure 4.4 shows the investment levels for the different scenarios. The internal funds are given, while the exploration activities are the decisions of the firm, with the constraint that the firm cannot invest more than the available internal funds. I am also assuming that, given the constraint, the

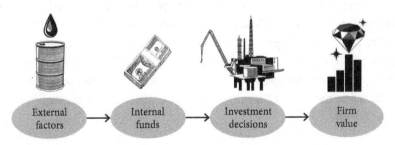

Figure 4.2 Framework for value creation

Oil price	Internal Funds to Invest
Oil price ↑	$300
Oil price unchanged	$200
Oil price ↓	$100

Exploration	NPV
$100	$20
$200	**$40**
$300	$30

Figure 4.3 Assumptions for example

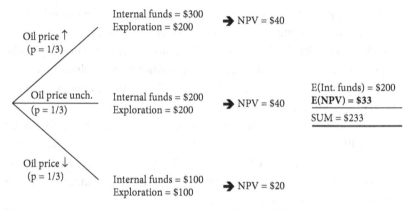

Figure 4.4 Investments and value with varied internal funds

management is behaving optimally.[1] If the probabilities of the three scenarios are the same, the expected NPV is ($40+$40+$20)/3 = $33.

Suppose instead that the oil price is stable at the current level. Then the internal funds would be $200, which, if invested, would yield an NPV of $40. Notice that while the expected internal funds would be the same as before, that is ($300+$200+$100)/3 also equals $200, the NPV is now $7 higher. The lower NPV with the uncertain oil price is attributable to the low internal funds when the oil price decreases, which leads to underinvestment and a lower NPV.

[1] If managers acted to line their own pockets, they might spend whatever funds they have, in which case the points I am trying to make with this example would only get stronger.

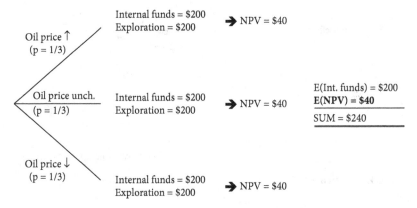

Figure 4.5 Investments and value with constant internal funds

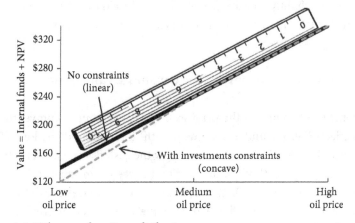

Figure 4.6 Value as a function of oil price

Another way of thinking about this problem is that the firm engages in hedging (in this case a costless hedge), such that it effectively locks in the oil price at the current level. In that case, the internal funds (when accounting for the hedging) is $200 irrespective of the oil price. Figure 4.5 shows this. That further means that the firm can invest at the optimal level in all three scenarios, and the expected NPV is $40.

Risk destroys value here because the investment constraint induces concavity in the value function. Figure 4.6 illustrates. Without the investment constraint, the firm would invest $200 in all scenarios, and the value function is linear. But when we introduce the investment constraint that the firm

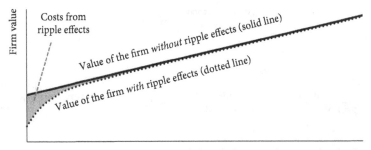

Figure 4.7 Concave value function

could not invest more than the internal funds, the value function gets a kink and becomes slightly concave (I have sought the aid of a ruler to emphasize the kink). This concavity explains why hedging enhances value.

4.4 The concavity of the corporate value function

The benefit of hedging in the prior example came from circumventing the ripple effects (i.e., the underinvestment) if the internal funds are low. We can generalize this idea. Figure 4.7 shows how the cash flow contributes to firm value. Ordinarily, we think of the relation between firm value and cash flow as linear (see the solid line). That is, irrespective of what the cash flow is, an incremental dollar of cash flow will have the same effect on firm value. But the ripple effects change that. When the cash flow gets sufficiently far down, the ripple effects surface and take a toll on firm value. Thus, we end up with a concave value function (see the dotted line). If there is a chance that our cash flow will fall to the concave area of the value function, hedging has the potential to create value. So just like with the utility functions for individuals, *it is concavity that gives rise to risk aversion and the potential benefit of hedging.*

4.5 The possible downside of corporate hedging: Extending our example

Now let us alter our earlier example such that the NPV of the exploration activities depends on the prevailing oil price. Figure 4.8 shows the NPV for

Exploration	NPV		
	Oil price ↓	Oil price unch.	Oil price ↑
$100	**$20**	$30	$40
$200	$0	**$40**	$50
$300	–$20	$20	**$60**

Optimal investment levels

Figure 4.8 Revised assumptions

Figure 4.9 Revised investments and value with varied internal funds

different exploration levels and oil prices. The boldfaced numbers indicate the maximum NPV given the oil price. For example, if the oil price drops, exploration activities of $100, $200, and $300 yield NPVs of $20, $0, and –$20, respectively. The highest of these NPV is $20, and the optimal investment level at this oil price level is therefore $100.

The optimal investment level increases with the oil price, as we would expect. In fact, this new feature dramatically changes our example.

Figure 4.9 shows the optimal investments for the same oil price and internal funds as earlier, but the exploration levels and NPVs are different to reflect the table in Figure 4.8. Assuming optimal investments, the expected NPV is now $40.

If we introduce hedging to the example, such that the internal funds are locked in at $200 irrespective of the oil price, we get the diagram in Figure 4.10. The problem here is that we only have $200 to invest when the oil price increases, so we cannot invest as much as would be optimal. This reduces the NPV, and the expected NPV is $37, which is $3 lower than in the diagram in Figure 4.9.

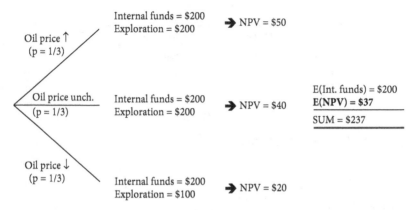

Figure 4.10 Revised investments and value with constant internal funds

What happened? In this example, the firm was what we call "naturally hedged." While the funds generated depended on the oil price, so did the investment opportunities. In other words, the firm generated substantial funds when it needed it the most, and it did not generate much funds when it did not need much. Introducing oil-price hedging in this example messed up a perfectly good natural hedge.

4.6 Does risk management affect optimal investment?

A common misconception is that risk management preserves the optimal investment levels in the face of changing commodity prices, such that, for example, an oil firm that has fixed the oil price for its output via hedging should keep investing the same irrespective of falling oil prices. Let us clear up this misconception before proceeding.

Suppose that an oil firm expects to produce 1 million barrels of oil at a cost of $50 per barrel. Given the current spot of $70 per barrel and a fixed cost of $5 million, the profit will be 1 million × ($70 – $50) – $5 million = $15 million. Further, suppose that the values of its investment projects correlate with commodity prices:

- Oil price = $80: NPV = $16 million
- Oil price = $70: NPV = $8 million
- Oil price = $60: NPV = –$2 million

The firm has the option to hedge by locking in an oil price of $70. If the firm enters this hedge and the oil price drops to $60, should it still invest?

The unhedged profit is 1 million × ($70 − $60) − $5 million = $5 million. Moreover, the hedging gain is 1 million × ($70 − $60) = $10 million and the NPV of the investment is −$2 million. Clearly, the company should just take the unhedged profit of $5 million and the hedging gain of $10 million for a total of $15 million, while rejecting the investment with a negative NPV. Thus, while some might argue that hedging allows the company to continue to invest when prices fall, the example illustrates that the investment and hedging decisions should be independent.

4.7 What firms benefit the most from risk management?

It is clear from the prior sections that the benefits of risk management vary widely, and that risk management even destroys value in certain circumstances. The firm characteristics that increase the chance that risk management creates value include the following:

- Risk factors:
  - o The firm's risk factors are easy to identify and measure. However, this is not the case for many firms. In particular, while it is reasonably easy to identify most risk factors, it can be very difficult to measure their potential impact on the firm. A later section discusses how we can identify and measure risk.
  - o The firm's risk factors can be managed effectively. Unfortunately, it is difficult to manage many risk factors, especially those that are unique to a firm. We will later partition the risk factors into categories and discuss how they can be managed.
- Ripple effects:[2]
  - o The firm is financially shaky, such that an adverse change in a risk factor is nontrivial and triggers substantial ripple effects.
  - o The firm has large financial distress costs. For example, if an airline suffers from financial distress, it can have devastating effects on its business. One effect is that potential customers avoid the airline because of concerns that safety is compromised or accumulated airline miles are rendered worthless in the future.

---

[2] See also the section in Chapter 2 on which companies exhibit the greatest ripples.

o The firm is opaque. An opaque firm generally faces greater costs when raising external funds, because investors are more concerned that they will be fooled. This is especially the case when the firm is financially shaky.

o The firm has strong investment opportunities. The opportunity cost of not being able to fund those investment opportunities is naturally great.

4.8 Different types of risk

For our purposes, risk can be partitioned into the following:

- market risk (also called systematic risk),
- commodity risk, and
- firm-specific risk (also called idiosyncratic risk).

As a general argument, it does not matter what the type of risk is, provided it affects cash flow and cash levels. But one could argue that the magnitude of some ripple effects depends on the type of risk. When a firm is cash-strapped because of a weak economy or commodity prices, it is likely that peer firms are also struggling. In such circumstances, it would be particularly difficult to (i) obtain external financing at reasonable terms, because the aggregate demand for financing is large; or (ii) sell assets at an acceptable price, because there are others selling but few with the means to buy. An analogy is trying to get a lifeboat when everybody's jumping ship, like when the *Titanic* was sinking. Or losing your job when the entire economy is in a recession, as Figure 4.11 illustrates. Thus, market risk and commodity risk are potentially

Figure 4.11 Job loss during a recession

more detrimental to firms than firm-specific risk. That is, market and commodity risks have a higher potential for *systemicity*.

4.9 The perspectives of equityholders vs. debtholders

Our discussion so far has implicitly assumed a total firm perspective. That is, we have examined whether risk affects total firm value. But I also pointed out that managers should maximize equity value, not total firm value. The question then is whether equityholders and debtholders have diverging risk preferences.

Figure 4.12 shows the total firm value partitioned into debt and equity values, albeit in an overly simplified way. If the total firm value is less than the face value of debt, the debt value equals the total firm value and the equity value is zero. If the total firm value exceeds the face value of debt, the debt value equals the face value and the equity value equals the total firm value less the face value of debt.

The equity value in the diagram looks like a call option (which I discuss in a later chapter), where the exercise price is the face value of debt. Indeed, an equity position can be viewed as an option on the firm. And just like a call option, the equity value function is *convex*, such that the equity value *increases* with risk.[3]

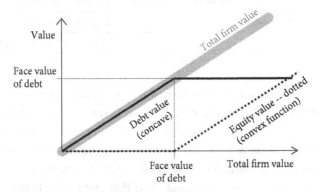

Figure 4.12 Total firm value partitioned into debt and equity

---

[3] It is also worth noting that, in reality, the equity value would be slightly positive even when the total firm value is less than the face value of debt, just like an out-of-the money call option has some value because of the possibility that the underlying asset value will increase before maturity.

In contrast, the debt value in the diagram looks like a short put option, and it is *concave*, such that the debt value *decreases* with risk.

Consider an example based on the balance sheet below. If the firm is liquidated today, the bondholders get $200, while the shareholders get nothing.

	Book value	Market value		Book value	Market value
Cash	$200	$200	LT bonds	$300	?
Fixed assets	$400	$0	Equity	$300	?
Total assets	$600	$200	Total L&E	$600	$200

The firm can inflate the risk by taking on a risky project at a cost of $200 (all of the firm's cash). The project has a present value of either $1,000 with 10% probability or nothing with 90% probability. Note that the project has a negative NPV and will destroy overall firm value. The values of the bonds and the shares are given in the table below. Without the risky project, the shareholders are certain to get nothing; with the risky project, the shareholders have a 10% chance of getting $700, at an expected value of $70. Clearly, it is in shareholders' interest to take on this project, even though it hurts overall firm value.

	Without risky project	With risky project
Value of bonds	$200	$300 × .1 = $30
Value of equity	$0	($1,000—$300) × .1 = $70

It is tempting to conclude that shareholders should use their influence to inflate the risk of levered firms. And this certainly happens, especially for firms that are in financial distress, in which case the total firm value hovers around the face value of debt, where the equity value function is most convex. But debtholders understand this incentive. Thus, they require covenants that constrain risk-taking. And they demand a higher interest rate if they fear that the firm will be risky in the future. Thus, it is not clear that it is wise for equityholders to "steal" from debtholders by inflating risk, and we might revert to the perspective of maximizing total value, because that also maximizes equity value. At least that is the general perspective that this book adopts.

4.10 The perspective of managers

Like other individuals, managers seek to maximize their own utility and are inherently risk averse (though it can be argued that the self-selection of individuals into managerial positions results in managers that have utility functions that are less concave than that of most individuals). How does that reconcile with a manager's job to maximize shareholder value?

This is a difficult question to answer because managers have multiple stakes in the companies for which they work, as Figure 4.13 illustrates. First and foremost, they have invested substantial human capital in their job that cannot readily be diversified. Generally, that job, and the accompanying salary, is more secure if the company is less risky. Moreover, it is likely that the working conditions are less stressful if the company is less risky. On this basis, managers likely prefer *less* risk than diversified shareholders.

Second, managers might have debt positions via their pensions. Our earlier discussion on the preference of debtholders suggests that they prefer low risk. Thus, pension benefits likely tilt managers toward preferring *less* risk.

Third, managers generally have an equity position in the firm in the form of shares and stock options. A common belief is that giving equity to managers

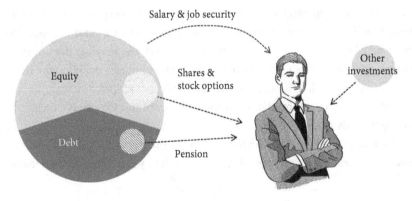

Figure 4.13 The multiple stakes of a manager

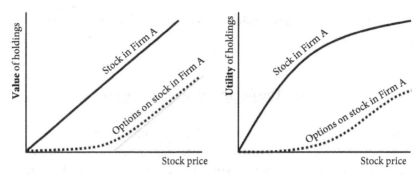

Figure 4.14 The value and utility of managers' stock and stock options

serves to align the interests of managers and shareholders. But unlike most shareholders, managers cannot readily diversify their stock holdings and hold substantial firm-specific risk for which they are not compensated. Thus, managers with many shares might prefer *less* firm-specific risk than do other shareholders.

Figure 4.14 illustrates the effect of managerial risk preferences.[4] The value function for stock is linear in the stock price, meaning that it is neither convex nor concave. The value function for options is convex, especially when the stock price is close to the exercise price. Managers who cannot diversify their stock and option positions will maximize the utility from the positions. Thus, the second graph transforms the values to utility, assuming a concave utility function. The stock graph clearly becomes concave, indicating that managers with undiversified stock positions prefer less risk. The option graph is now more linear, and whether it is convex or concave depends on the relative strength of the convexity of the original option value and the concavity of the utility function. It will likely retain its convexity close to the exercise price and become concave when it is far in-the-money, which is how the graph is drawn. If so, granting at-the-money stock options to executives induces them to take more risk. Interestingly, that risk incentive vanishes as the stock price increases, so the executives must be awarded more at-the-money options to preserve their risk-taking incentives.

Overall, managers likely prefer that the company is exposed to less risk than what most shareholders prefer. This tendency is intensified by pension

---

[4] If you are not familiar with stock options and value graphs for stock options, you might want to skip ahead and read the initial parts of the chapter on options before returning to the rest of this section.

benefits and undiversified stock holdings in the firm, but probably offset by at-the-money option holdings.

4.11 Selective hedging

Managers often practice selective hedging based on their view of future price movements. That is, managers increase hedging activities when they believe that commodity prices will move in their disfavor and scale back hedging activities when they believe that commodity prices will move in their favor.

Managers presumably practice selective hedging because they are confident in their ability to predict price changes. As noted earlier, people are generally overconfident, for example, 70% believe they are better-than-average drivers. And executives are probably particularly over-confident because of self-selection (confident people are more likely to seek positions of leadership) and past professional success. They might even see themselves as superheroes who cannot fail, like the one in Figure 4.15.

Figure 4.15 An overconfident manager

Like investors who engage in technical trading, managers might believe that they can detect patterns in prices even if there are none. Indeed, we have an inherent tendency to search for patterns around us. Random sequences exhibit natural clustering (e.g., in commodity prices following a random walk), and such clustering often appears to be nonrandom. For example, the "random" shuffle on the original iPods was adjusted so it appears to be "more random." The original and truly random order of songs produced substantial repetition (the same song or artist played consecutively), such that the listener believed the shuffling was nonrandom. According to Steve Jobs, the algorithm was changed to be "less random to make it feel more random."

However, it is questionable whether managers are at much of an advantage, if any, in predicting future commodity prices. If so, they should be trading commodities instead. One could argue that if managers lack an edge in predicting prices, selective hedging is innocuous. A more pessimistic view is that selective hedging gets in the way of hedging for the right reasons and is therefore harmful. For example, managers are often wary of hedging after a commodity price drop, because they think that the price will recover. But it is often after such a price drop that future firm prospects are dim and the need for hedging to mitigate ripple effects is dire. Relying on a bet that the price will recover can be detrimental in such circumstances.

4.12 An example of flawed selective hedging

An article titled "Oil Fims Lock In Current Prices" published in the *Wall Street Journal* on April 25, 2016, provides a good illustration of the fallacies of selective hedging. At that time, the WTI crude price was only $42. The article states that EV Energy Partners LP selected not to hedge the prior spring when the prices were between $50 and $60 (which was much less than in prior years), and quoted their finance chief as saying "We thought we were smarter than everyone -- lessons learned." Apparently, they selected not to hedge because they thought prices would rebound, but instead the prices declined further.

The article also states that "Continental Resources Inc., one of the biggest U.S. shale drillers, famously closed out most of its oil hedges in late 2014 when oil first traded below $80 a barrel, betting prices would quickly rise

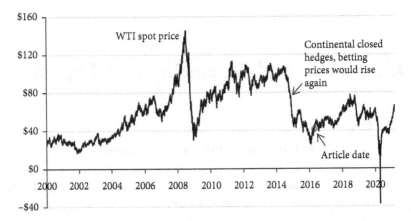

Figure 4.16 Oil prices over time

again. The decision cost the company tens of millions of dollars as prices continued to plunge. Continental declined to comment."

As a context, Figure 4.16 shows WTI oil prices from 2010 to 2020 and denotes when Continental Resources Inc. closed its hedge, because it was "betting prices would quickly rise again."

5

Identifying and Measuring Risk Exposure

5.1 Direct and indirect risk exposure

Commodity prices can affect a firm's cash flow directly or indirectly. Direct price exposure refers to the immediate effect and is relatively easy to identify and measure. A couple of examples illustrate.

- A jeweler uses primarily silver to make jewelry. If the silver price increases by 10%, the cost of raw material increases by 10%.
- Ford sells cars to Spain. If the euro drops in value by 10%, Ford's dollar revenues from the sales to Spain also drop by 10% (at least as the most immediate effect).

But the overall exposure is more convoluted, and there might be different types of indirect exposure. For simplicity I lump all exposure that is not direct exposure in a broad category of indirect exposure. First, firms can take actions to mitigate direct exposure. Let us consider some mitigating factors in our two examples:

- The jeweler might
  o change input to other materials such as stainless steel, or
  o pass on the increased costs to customers as higher prices.
- Ford might
  o increase euro car prices, or
  o move manufacturing to the Eurozone.

(Naturally, the actions above have yet other consequences. For example, increasing prices could lower demand, while moving manufacturing could change product quality.)

Second, commodity prices might affect multiple aspects of the landscape in which the firm operates, which, in turn, affect the firm's cash flow. For example, Ford could suffer from a depreciation in the yen even in the absence of direct exposure. Specifically, if the yen depreciates, Japanese manufacturers

Applied Corporate Risk and Liquidity Management. Erik Lie, Oxford University Press. © Oxford University Press 2023. DOI: 10.1093/oso/9780197664995.003.0005

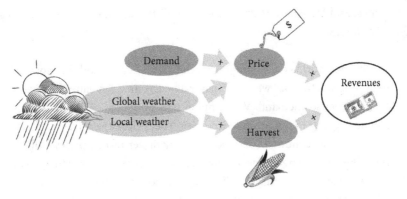

Figure 5.1 Natural hedge in farming

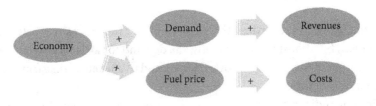

Figure 5.2 Natural hedge in the airline industry

might decrease their euro prices, making Japanese cars more competitively priced than Ford in Spain and, thus, stealing market share from Ford.

Third, commodity prices might correlate with other parts of the business. Farming represents a good example. Figure 5.1 illustrates. A corn farmer's revenues depend on corn yield and corn prices. Both the yield and the prices depend on the weather, with the difference that the farmer's yield depends on local weather, whereas prices primarily depend on the "global" weather that affects most corn farmers. For the major corn-producing states, the local and global weather overlap, such that corn prices and yield correlate. In Iowa, Illinois, and Indiana, the correlation between corn prices and yield is about −0.50. Thus, a price decrease is generally offset by a yield increase, and vice versa. In other words, farmers are naturally hedged against changes in corn prices. Incidentally, this also pertains to businesses that depend on farmers/farming, such as Deere & Company.

The airline industry offers another example where commodity prices correlate with the quantity of products/services (in this case, air fares) sold, such that there is a natural hedge in place against price increases. Figure 5.2

illustrates, and US Airways President Scott Kirby summarized this idea in a 2012 conference:

> I think a non-fuel hedging program is the most effective and the most rational program because we have a natural hedge. This is a natural hedge—fuel prices versus demand. When fuel prices are going up, in most cases revenue is going to follow and vice-versa. Fuel prices are driven in many regards by the economy. That's not the only driver of fuel prices, but it's probably—over a longer time horizon, it is the principal driver of fuel prices as what's happening with the economy, and so we have a strong natural hedge. And if we hedge jet fuel prices or hedge oil prices, you're breaking this natural hedge, not to mention the expense of hedging but just the natural hedge that you have between jet fuel and revenues.

In other words, to the extent that increases in jet fuel prices are fueled (pun intended) by a boost in the economy, the demand for airfares also increases, such that both revenues and costs increase and the net effect on earnings and cash flow is modest.

In sum, indirect commodity price exposure is complicated. But we have at least identified the following factors to be relevant:

- The pricing flexibility, which depends on demand elasticity and the behavior of competitors.
- The ability to shift production and sourcing inputs.
- The extent to which investment opportunities depend on commodity prices. In an earlier section, we saw this for an oil company whose NPV of exploration opportunities depended on oil prices.
- The extent to which the quantity produced is correlated with commodity prices, as we saw for the corn farmer and the airline industry.

5.2 Measuring risk exposure via simulations

One possible way to measure overall risk measure is to run simulations. The basic idea is to run a simulation of a firm's cash flow/level while holding the commodity price of interest constant, and then repeat the simulation while allowing the commodity price to vary. We can then compare the distributions of the cash flow/level from the two simulations to gauge the incremental effect of the commodity exposure. Figure 5.3 shows an example of such a comparison.

While this procedure has some intuitive appeal, it also has some drawbacks. Most critically, the simulation depends heavily on our ability to correctly identify the various ways in which commodity prices affect cash flow and, thus, cash levels. The direct exposure is relatively easy, but the indirect exposure can be very challenging.

Figure 5.4 illustrates the effect of indirect exposure. The graph shows the simulated cash flows for an airline for which revenues increase with the economic conditions, while the economic conditions and fuel prices are assumed to either be (1) unrelated or (2) positively related, that is, fuel prices tend to be high when the economy is strong. We see that the case with the positive correlation between the economy and fuel prices gives a narrower cash flow distribution, because the positive correlation works like a natural hedge.

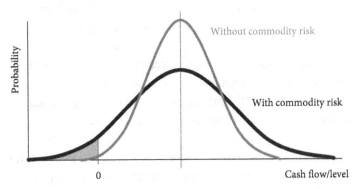

Figure 5.3 Cash distributions with and without commodity risk

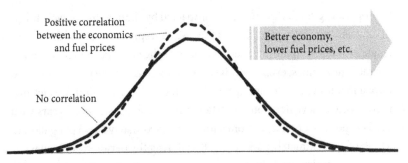

Figure 5.4 The effect of indirect exposure on cash flow distribution

5.3 Measuring risk exposure via regressions

An alternative method to measure risk exposure is to regress past cash flow changes against past commodity price changes. If changes in commodity prices affect cash flow, the regressions should reveal that.

A problem with cash flow regressions is that cash flows are quite "noisy," in the sense that they are driven by many factors beyond commodity prices. Thus, we need a relatively large sample of observations to disentangle the effects. Unfortunately, we generally have cash flow data only on a quarterly basis, so even if we use, say five years of data, we only have 20 observations. Running regressions with so few and noisy observations yields imprecise results.

To increase the number of observations in the regressions, we can substitute stock returns for cash flow changes and use daily data. A few caveats apply:

- Stock returns reflect both current and future cash flow, and the results should be interpreted accordingly.
- Stock returns are exacerbated by leverage, such that the relation between stock returns and commodity prices will be stronger for firms with great leverage.
- The regression implicitly assumes that the capital market understands how commodity prices affect cash flow and value. (In other words, we assume that the capital market is efficient in reflecting this information.)
- Stock returns are only available for publicly traded firms.

The advantage to a stock return regression is that it is very easy to run. To illustrate, I ran a regression for American Airlines (AA) to gauge its exposure to jet fuel prices. For a bit more background, AA reported the following in its 2015 10K:

Our operating results are materially impacted by changes in the availability, price volatility and cost of aircraft fuel, which represents one of the largest single cost items in our business. Because of the amount of fuel needed to operate our airlines, even a relatively small increase in the price of fuel can have a material adverse aggregate effect on our costs and liquidity. Jet fuel market prices have fluctuated substantially over the past several years with market spot prices ranging from a low of approximately $1.55 per gallon to a high of approximately $3.37 per gallon during the period from January 1, 2011 to December 31, 2014.

During the second quarter of 2014, we sold our portfolio of fuel hedging contracts that were scheduled to settle on or after June 30, 2014. We have not entered into any transactions to hedge our fuel consumption since December 9, 2013 and, accordingly, as of December 31, 2014, we did not have any fuel hedging contracts outstanding. As such, and assuming we do not enter into any future transactions to hedge our fuel consumption, we will continue to be fully exposed to fluctuations in fuel prices.

I first downloaded daily stock prices for AA, daily levels for the S&P 500 index (as a proxy for the market portfolio), and daily jet fuel prices from 2006 to 2014. Then I organized the data and estimated daily returns for all three data items. All my regressions are based on returns (and <u>not prices</u>) such that the daily observations are scaled and independent (which follows from a random walk). Figure 5.5 shows how I did this in Excel.

Then I estimated the correlations between the variables. These are presented in the correlation matrix below. Notice that the S&P 500 returns are positively correlated with both the American Airlines returns and the jet fuel returns. This has implications for the regressions below.

	AAL	S&P 500	Jet Fuel
AAL	1	0.48	−0.02
S&P 500	0.48	1	0.33
Jet Fuel	−0.02	0.33	1

I ran three regressions, all with the stock returns as the dependent (Y) variable:

1. The S&P 500 returns as the only independent (X) variable.
2. The jet fuel returns as the only independent (X) variable.
3. The S&P 500 returns and the jet fuel returns as independent (X) variables.

▲	A	B	C	D	E	F	G	H
1		Prices				Returns		
2	Date	AAL	S&P 500	Jet Fuel		AAL	S&P 500	Jet Fuel
3	38720	37.26	1268.8	1.819				
4	38721	39	1273.46	1.855		=B4/B3-1	=C4/C3-1	=D4/D3-1
5	38722	39.51	1273.48	1.813		=B5/B4-1	=C5/C4-1	=D5/D4-1

Figure 5.5 Calculations of returns in Excel

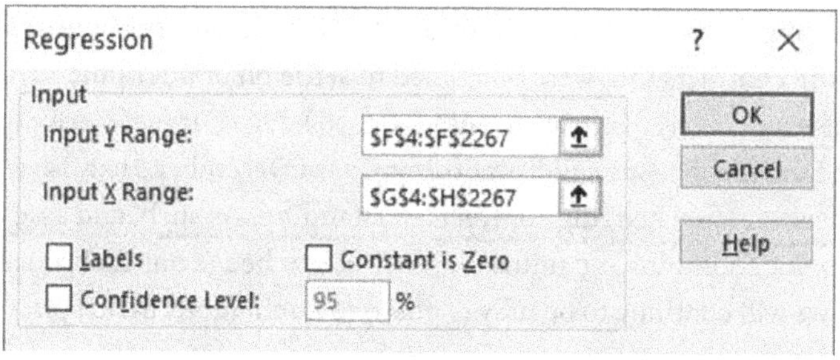

Figure 5.6 Selecting data for the regression

To run the regressions, I selected *Regression* from *Data Analysis* in the *Data* menu and highlighted the cells with the return data, as illustrated in Figure 5.6.

The results are shown below. (I have removed some of the standard output from the regressions, labeled the X variables, and altered the number formatting.) In the first regression, the S&P 500 coefficient is 1.773. This is an estimate of AA's stock beta, and suggests that AA's stock moves, on average, 1.8% for a 1% change in the market portfolio.

In the second regression, the jet fuel coefficient is –0.036, but its p-value is as high as 0.437, suggesting that the coefficient is not statistically different from zero. (To be statistically significant at the 1% level, a common benchmark, the p-value would have to be below 0.01.) Thus, we have no reliable evidence that the stock returns are linked to jet fuel returns. What is going on here? Does this mean that AA is not exposed to jet fuel prices?

	Regression 1		Regression 2		Regression 3	
R Square	0.230		0.000		0.264	
Observations	2,264		2,264		2,264	
	Coefficient	P-value	Coefficient	P-value	Coefficient	P-value
Intercept	0.001	0.367	0.001	0.188	0.001	0.345
S&P 500	1.773	0.000			2.013	0.000
Jet Fuel			–0.036	0.437	–0.431	0.000

This is a case of *omitted variable bias*, which is a major concern in all kinds of studies. For example, suppose that we wanted to know whether listening to

Mozart as a baby improves academic performance. One way to test this would be to ask a large sample of individuals about their college grades and whether they were exposed to Mozart as babies. Then we could regress the college grades against a dummy variable that captures Mozart exposure. My guess is that the regression would reveal a strong positive relation, that is, individuals who were exposed to Mozart as babies get better grades. However, this analysis potentially ignores an important tendency for parents of babies who listen to Mozart to be high achievers. If so, the individuals who listened to Mozart as babies might simply have inherited high-achieving genes. To disentangle the Mozart effect from the genetic effect, we could include the college grades or IQ scores of the parents in the regression as an additional variable. I expect that we would see that the coefficient on the college grades or IQ scores of the parents would be positive and strong, and the Mozart coefficient would be much weaker and perhaps statistically insignificant. Another example is the World Health Organization's (WHO) recent exoneration of coffee as a risk factor for cancer based on an examination of recent studies. Why might earlier studies have indicated a risk? One likely reason is that coffee consumption, at least some years ago, tended to go hand in hand with smoking. Thus, to examine the effect of coffee, it is critical to control for smoking.[1]

Omitted variable bias arises when we exclude a relevant variable that is correlated with the independent variable of interest. In our AA example, the correlation coefficient between the S&P 500 returns and the jet fuel returns is 0.33. As a result, the jet fuel returns pick up some of the S&P 500 return effect when the S&P 500 returns are omitted from the regression.

Let us see what happens when we include both the S&P 500 returns and the jet fuel returns as independent variables. The jet fuel coefficient is now –0.431 and statistically significant (the p-value is less than 0.01), while the S&P 500 coefficient increases to 2.013 and is still statistically significant. In other words, the market and jet fuel prices have opposing effects on AA's equity value, consistent with what the US Airways president explained about airlines' exposure to the economy and jet fuel prices. Figure 5.7 illustrates these complex relations.

[1] There are plenty of other correlations that we should be cautious to interpret. Personally, I have witnessed during countless trips to the pool that the swimmers who take lessons are the worst, so one might conclude that swim lessons are useless. Or how about the positive correlation that exists between almond consumption and health—does this necessarily imply that almonds are good for your health?

Figure 5.7 The relations between stock market prices, airline stock prices, and fuel prices

Another illustration of omitted variable bias is to examine the effect of sugar prices on the value of a random company, such as Microsoft Corp (ticker MSFT) as a former student of mine did. There should be no economic effect here, so it can be viewed as a placebo (or "sugar pill"—get it?) test. But it turns out that sugar prices are positively correlated with the economy; the correlation between the returns of SGG (an ETF for sugar) and the returns on the S&P 500 is close to 20%. Thus, a regression of MSFT returns against SGG returns yields a positive coefficient that differs statistically from zero (i.e., the p-value is less than 0.01). But if we control for S&P 500 returns, the statistical significance of the effect of sugar prices on Microsoft disappears (i.e., the p-value is 0.143).

Let us return to the AA regressions. R^2 also provides valuable information about risk exposure. In general, R^2 provides the fraction of the variance in the dependent variable that can be explained by the independent variables. (R provides the fraction of the standard deviation in the dependent variable that can be explained by the independent variables, but standard deviations are not additive, so I focus on R^2 here.) In the first regression for AA, R^2 is 0.230, meaning that 23% of the variance of AA's stock returns is attributable to the market. In the third regression, R^2 increases to 0.264, which means that the incremental $0.264-0.230 = 0.034$ is attributable to jet fuel. The remaining $1-0.264 = 73.6\%$ is unexplained by the regression model, and it can be categorized as the firm-specific part of the variance. The pie chart in Figure 5.8 illustrates this.

What can AA do to reduce risk? Hedging jet fuel prices by itself would have no value, as recognized by the US Airways president. But hedging both systematic risk and jet fuel prices (in different directions) should be effective, and this is seemingly a possibility that the US Airways president failed to recognize or simply ignored.

Fractions of Variance

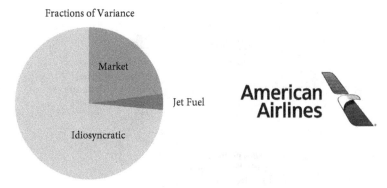

Figure 5.8 The fractions of variance for AA's stock returns

Another interesting case is that of United Parcel Service (UPS). UPS has substantial fuel costs, and one might guess that its performance and value would be hurt by increasing oil prices. But a regression analysis of how its stock price depends on the market and the oil price from 2015 to 2017 shows that its market beta is 0.85 and highly statistically significant, whereas its oil beta is statistically insignificant. Thus, the value of UPS depends on the performance of the overall economy, but not on oil prices. Why might this be? A likely explanation is that UPS passes on increases in the cost from rising oil prices to its customers. Another possibility is that it hedges its exposure. An excerpt from its 2016 annual report suggests that both are true, and especially the former:

> We are exposed to changes in the prices of refined fuels, principally jet-A, diesel and unleaded gasoline, as well as changes in the price of natural gas. Currently, the fuel surcharges that we apply to our domestic and international package and LTL services are the primary means of reducing the risk of adverse fuel price changes. Additionally, we periodically use a combination of option, forward and futures contracts to provide partial protection from changing fuel and energy prices.

5.4 The components of total risk

The airline regression example showed that systematic risk is a greater component of risk than commodity price risk, even for a company that is heavily dependent on a commodity for its operations. This pattern can be

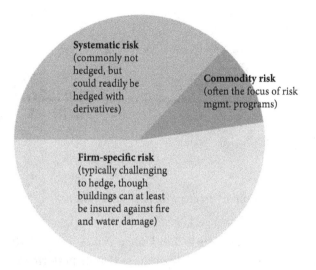

Figure 5.9 Partitioning of firm risk

generalized to other firms; firm-specific risk generally represents the largest component of total risk, followed by market risk, and then commodity risk. Figure 5.9 illustrates this.

In an earlier section, I argued that market risk and commodity risk are potentially more harmful to firms than idiosyncratic risk, because the two former risk factors produce greater ripple effects. Does this imply that firms should focus more on hedging market and commodity risks? Perhaps. But that also depends on the costs and availability of various hedging mechanisms.

Beyond buying insurance on buildings and equipment, it is difficult to hedge firm-specific risk. In contrast, there are various derivatives that are readily available and well suited for hedging market risk and commodity risk. The next sections discuss these risk management tools.

Corporate risk management programs tend to focus on mitigating commodity risk. The lack of attention given to market risk is curious considering the discussion above and other factors. Let us review some arguments for why market risk should be hedged:

- Market risk tends to constitute a larger portion of overall risk than commodity risk. (The COVID-19 pandemic is a chilling example of the devastating effect that systematic risk factors can have on the economy as a whole and for individual businesses.)

- Investors expect extra compensation to hold market risk, such that firms with more market risk face a higher cost of capital.
- The ripple effects from market risk are likely to be great due to *systemicity* (e.g., when you need to sell assets to raise funds, potential buyers are also in bad shape).
- Market risk is arguably easy to hedge using derivatives.

I will leave the lack of attention to market risk as an empirical puzzle. But *I strongly encourage readers to consider hedging market risk* for their own firms or the firms for which they are working.

Finally, a thought for you to ponder: In light of systemicity, would our firm be better off if all our peers hedge common risk factors?

5.5 Long versus short positions

Before we move to the hedging part, it is useful to discuss the terminology of long versus short positions (or "being long" versus "being short"). I use these terms later, and I have found that students get confused when I do.

A long position implies that we currently own the underlying asset. Thus, we benefit from an appreciation in the asset price. Examples of being long include investors who own stocks or bonds, oil companies that drill oil from their reserves, mining companies that mine minerals from their mines, farmers that harvest wheat from their fields, and exporters that receive foreign currency.

In contrast, a short position implies that we owe or need to acquire the underlying asset. Thus, we benefit from a depreciation in the asset price.

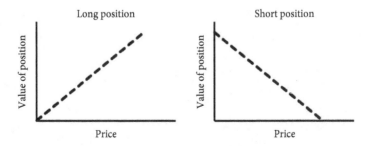

Figure 5.10 Long vs. short positions

Examples of being short include investors who have shorted stock (i.e., borrowed shares from their broker that they have sold, with the intention of buying the shares back later and returning them to their broker), airlines that buy jet fuel for their operations, car manufacturers that use steel for the production, and US firms that pay off Chinese suppliers in yuan. Figure 5.10 illustrates both a long position and a short position.

In general, hedging entails taking offsetting positions. That is, if a firm is long an asset, it needs to short that same (or similar) asset, for example, using derivatives, to reduce risk, and vice versa. The next sections, especially those on derivatives, discuss this in detail.

6

Managing Idiosyncratic Risk

6.1 Idiosyncratic risk

The bulk of a business's risk exposure is idiosyncratic. This chapter briefly discusses some of these risk factors, and what, if anything, can be done to reduce idiosyncratic risk. Think, for example, of the loss that VW suffered in both its reputation and value from its manipulation of emission tests. Or the loss that Samsung suffered when the batteries on the Galaxy Note 7 exploded. Guarding against such incidents goes beyond traditional risk management tools; it requires a culture of honesty, integrity, and transparency. And even that is not enough.

Property and liability risk can be reduced (though not eliminated) with insurance. And credit risk can be either avoided or at least partially mitigated. But this chapter offers no effective hedging mechanism for many other idiosyncratic risk factors, including reputational risk, operational risk, compliance risk, and regulatory risk. For example, the problems that afflicted VW and Samsung cannot be managed via commercial insurance due to information asymmetries and incentive misalignments (which we refer to as *adverse selection* and *moral hazard* below).

In fact, I contend that only a sliver of idiosyncratic risk can be reduced with insurance and attention to credit risk. Thus, we must accept most idiosyncratic risk and construct a suitable buffer instead. Such a buffer could come in the form of a cash cushion and limited debt burden. The later chapters on payout policy and capital structure are particularly relevant in this regard.

6.2 Property and liability risk

Most companies own substantial property, including buildings, equipment, and inventory, and this property is susceptible to direct and indirect losses from fire, theft, burst water pipes, etc. If, for example, a factory is destroyed by fire, the *direct loss* is the deterioration in value of the factory, while the *indirect loss* is the lost profits from the production interruption.

Applied Corporate Risk and Liquidity Management. Erik Lie, Oxford University Press. © Oxford University Press 2023.
DOI: 10.1093/oso/9780197664995.003.0006

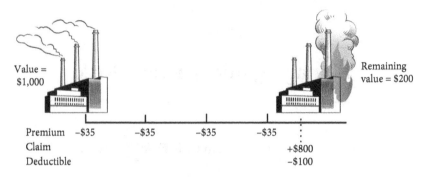

Figure 6.1 Insurance payout following factory fire

In addition, companies are exposed to potential loss from legal liability arising from intentional or unintentional torts. Such liability risk includes employers' liability and workers' compensation (for, e.g., work injuries), automobile liability, and general liability (such as serving coffee that is so hot that it causes burn injuries).

To mitigate property and liability risk, companies can buy property and liability insurance. The insurance policy stipulates what is covered, what perils give rise to a claim, any deductible, any coinsurance, any policy limit, the price (called insurance premium), and other terms. Suppose that Widget Inc. insures a factory with a value of $1,000 for $35 per year. In the middle of the fourth year, the factory catches fire, and the remaining value is deemed to be $200, as shown in Figure 6.1. In other words, the firm suffers a loss of $800 (assuming no indirect losses for simplicity), which is also the amount of the insurance claim. With a deductible of $100, the firm receives $700 from the insurance company. Incidentally, if the probability of a fire (or other peril) is 5% each year and the expected payment from the insurance company in that case is $700, then the premium of $35 is said to be *actuarially fair* (because $35 = 5% × $700).

6.3 Challenges with insurance: Adverse selection and moral hazard

Not all idiosyncratic risk factors are insurable—ideally, the following holds:

- There are many fairly homogenous exposure units, such as buildings or cars. This facilitates the estimation of future losses based on historical data and, thereby, the pricing of the insurance. In addition, it allows the insurance company to diversify its risk across units.

- Any loss is clear and measurable, such that it is immune (or at least less susceptible) to disagreement and fraud. For example, during the COVID-19 pandemic, restaurateurs and retailers sued their insurers for refusing to cover billions of dollars in business losses because the insurance companies refused to cover the losses. Insurance policies often exclude viruses and typically require physical damage, but the argument was made that the coronavirus remains on physical surfaces and renders the facilities unsafe.

- The insurer and the insured have access to the same information about the exposure units. This minimizes *adverse selection*, in which managers of firms choose to insure only exposure units that are most likely to produce a large insurance payoff (just like unhealthy individuals are more inclined to purchase health insurance than healthy individuals).

- Any loss is accidental and beyond the control of the insured. This minimizes *moral hazard*, in which managers of the insured firm inflate the risk at the expense of the insurance company. (People tend to behave more recklessly, such as exceeding speed limits, when they know their actions have limited downsides, e.g., because they are insured.)

Large deviations from these ideal characteristics imply that insurance is not feasible. Small deviations generally lead to higher insurance premiums or altered terms. I will elaborate on the problems of adverse selection and moral hazard.

Adverse selection

Let us revisit the insurance example above. Suppose that Widget Inc. has two buildings it might insure, one with a probability of fire (or other peril) of 4% and another with a probability of 6%. But the buildings look identical to outsiders, and the insurance premiums are the same. In that case, Widget would definitely insure the latter building (with a premium below what is actuarially fair), but perhaps not the first (with a premium above what is actuarially fair). The annual expected insurance payoff is then $6\% \times \$700 = \$42$, which exceeds the insurance premium. Thus, the insurance company must raise premiums to make a profit, perhaps so much that Widget might choose not to insure any factories, or perhaps just factories with an even higher probability of fire. The end result of such adverse selection is that insurance premiums soar and only the riskiest assets are insured, or, in the worst case, the insurance market collapses.

Adverse selection is especially prominent for health insurance, as Figure 6.2 illustrates. Individuals with preexisting conditions or unhealthy habits are more inclined to purchase health insurance than healthy individuals, and they are likely to conceal these conditions and habits. While the insurance companies might not observe the conditions and habits, they recognize the inclinations of unhealthy individuals to buy insurance and will raise the insurance premiums for everyone, healthy or unhealthy.

One way to reduce adverse selection is for the insurance company to gather more information (like they do for individuals who seek life insurance). However, information gathering is costly, and the costs are ultimately borne by the insured customers via higher premiums. Another way to reduce adverse selection is via *screening*, in which the insurance company structures the terms to weed out high-risk assets, for example, by using a

Figure 6.2 Adverse selection in health insurance

Figure 6.3 Moral hazard in car insurance

high deductible. The idea is that insurance customers are reluctant to accept high deductibles on high-risk assets, because the deductible has a larger expected effect on the payoff.[1]

Moral hazard

The car insurance market is useful to gain the intuition for moral hazard. Individuals with comprehensive car insurance are likely to behave more recklessly, for example, by exceeding speed limits and leaving the car out in hailstorms, because they believe that their actions have limited downsides. Figure 6.3 illustrates this. The insurance company could try to monitor and change behavior by placing tracking devices in the car, perhaps in exchange for lower premiums. But such tracking devices can be costly and present privacy concerns.

Let us return to the example with Widget Inc. Suppose that Widget Inc. has a system of routines and equipment in place at its factory at an annual

---

[1] An intriguing example of screening involves the rock band Van Halen. Their elaborate touring contract specified that the local hosts supply a bowl of M&Ms but "absolutely no brown ones." A casual look at the food and beverages gave a good indicator of whether the local hosts had read and adhered to the contract, including the more important technical and security specifications that were crucial to the spectacular live show.

cost of $4 that reduces the probability of a fire (or other peril) by 2%. The expected benefit per year is 2% × $800 = $16, thus suggesting that the system generates a positive value of $12 per year. If the factory is uninsured, Widget keeps this value for itself, and has a strong incentive to retain the system. But what happens if Widget insures the factory? Most of the benefit from the system accrues to the insurance company. Widget's benefit is the reduced probability of incurring the deductible of $100, so the expected benefit per year is only 2% × $100 = $2, not quite enough to justify the cost of $4. We end up with a socially suboptimal situation in which Widget will ditch the system and the insurance company might not find it profitable to provide insurance anymore.

What can the insurance company do to incentivize Widget to retain the system? One possibility is to offer a reduced premium on the condition that Widget retains the system, but this requires additional monitoring. Another possibility is to raise the deductible to at least $200 to give Widget more "skin in the game," thereby raising Widget's expected benefit per year to at least 2% × $200 = $4.

Overall, we see that the world of insurance is full of challenges. Some of these challenges can be solved with greater information gathering, monitoring, deductibles, and co-insurance. However, information-gathering and monitoring are costly, and the purchasers of insurance end up paying for those costs. Furthermore, deductibles and co-insurance effectively mean that the losses are not fully covered and that the insurance does not remove all risk. Figure 6.4 illustrates this. As a result, firms might optimally choose to forgo insurance, even if idiosyncratic risk harms firm value.

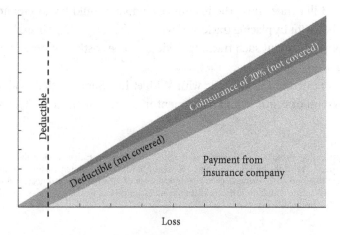

Figure 6.4 The effects of deductibles and coinsurance

6.4 Alternatives to commercial insurance: Self-insurance and corporate diversification

What if commercial insurance is unavailable or too expensive? There are certainly alternatives to buying commercial insurance. One alternative is simply to ignore the risk and hope for the best. Another alternative is to adopt some kind of self-insurance. That is, the firm could set aside funds for a rainy day. This works particularly well when the losses are expected to be small and scattered. For example, I do not buy a warranty when I purchase electronic goods, because the warranty is generally priced too high and I have the funds to repair or replace the items if something should happen. Thus, self-insurance can be thoughts of as precautionary cash holdings, which we discussed earlier.

Companies can also diversify the risk in various ways. For example, it can diversify its line of products or services, or across geographic areas. This can be accomplished via organic growth or acquisitions. However, diversification could deplete cash reserves that are kept for precautionary purposes. Also, diversification entails entering areas in which the management is likely to have less experience and expertise. Finally, diversification via acquisitions often occurs at a substantial premium to the stand-alone value. Thus, diversification, despite its best intentions, could end up *inflating* risk, and I would generally recommend against diversification as a corporate risk-management tool.

A creative example of managing unique risk comes from the mattress business. As a 2019 World Series promotion, Jim "Mattress Mack" McIngvale of Gallery Furniture in Houston offered customers who bought mattresses costing at least $3,000 a full refund if the Houston Astros won, as Figure 6.5

Figure 6.5 The curious relation between the mattress business and the Houston Astros

depicts. Of course, this was a very risky promotion for Mattress Mack. And no insurance companies would give him an acceptable rate to cover the potential loss of about $15 million. Instead, he enlisted the help of experienced sports bettors, who placed a series of large bets in Las Vegas, New Jersey, and Biloxi, Mississippi, for the Astros to win. Thus, while most use sports betting to gamble, Mattress Mack used it to reduce existing risk exposure.

6.5 Credit risk

Most businesses deal with credit risk, that is, the risk that customers fail to pay or counterparties fail to deliver on contractual obligations. Credit risk depends on the creditworthiness of the customer/counterparty, the size and maturity of the credit, the size and volatility of unrealized profits from the contractual position, the use of legally binding netting agreements, etc.

A company can obviously make allowances for bad debt losses. In addition, companies often engage in loss-prevention techniques to mitigate credit risk. This invariably entails assessing the creditworthiness of the customer/counterparty.

But how do you assess the creditworthiness and default probability of a trading partner? There are many dimensions to consider, including profitability (both the level and variability), leverage, and cash holdings. But you should be careful when interpreting these dimensions. For example, cash generally indicates financial strength. Thus, we would expect that firms with plenty of cash would have strong credit ratings. Indeed, many models designed to predict default, like Altman's Z, assume that the firms' likelihood of default decreases monotonically with cash.

However, consider the empirical relation between cash holdings and credit ratings in Figure 6.6. As expected, firms with an AAA rating have substantial cash. These are likely firms that accumulate cash simply as a result of being "cash cows." But firms with a C rating also have lots of cash. What is going on? Do we have to rethink the role of cash? The problem here is one of *endogeneity*. Imagine that you get to a part of the South Side of Chicago with lots of police officers on patrol. What would you think? One possibility is that this must be a very safe neighborhood, because police presence serves to combat crime. Another possibility is that this must be a crime-ridden neighborhood, which is why the police presence is so strong in the first place (and without the police presence, the crime might be even worse). The latter

Figure 6.6 The relation between firms' credit ratings and cash holdings

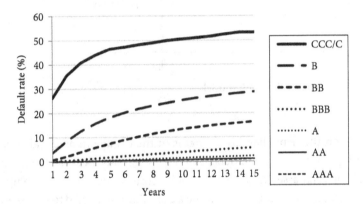

Figure 6.7 Average cumulative default rates

might also happen for cash—when firms are particularly shaky, executives try to save cash to stay afloat. Our analysis arrives at the same general conclusion, that is, when firms are financially weak, risk management and cash preservation are most valuable.

Credit rating companies like Moody's and S&P consider multiple dimensions when issuing bond ratings, and historical default rates for these bond ratings represent a reasonable measure of default probability. For example, based on Figure 6.7, the probability that a B-rated bond will default in the next two years is a little less than 9%.[2]

Structural models provide another approach. Under structural models, default occurs when the firm's asset value falls below a critical value that

---

[2] The data come from S&P's 2015 Annual Global Corporate Default Study and Rating Transitions.

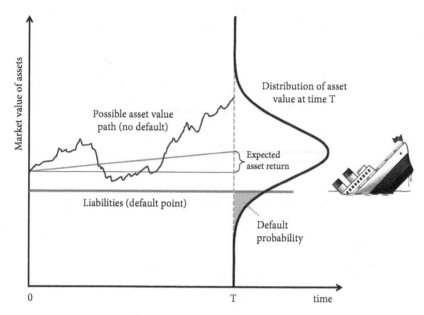

Figure 6.8 Structural default model

depends on the firm's liabilities. That is, if the change in asset value is sufficiently poor, the firm will default on its obligations, because the liabilities exceed the total asset value. Figure 6.8 illustrates this concept. The upward sloping, straight line indicates that the asset value is expected to increase over time, while the erratic line indicates the actual change in value over time. Because the erratic asset value line never falls below the default line, the firm does not default during this period. Naturally, there are other possible scenarios that could have occurred. If we assume a distribution for the possible asset values during the period, we can estimate the default probability (which is shaded in the graph).

Based on this general framework, it is possible to apply option-pricing theory to estimate the probability of default. That is, assuming that the asset value moves randomly around an expected path, we can estimate the probability that it will hit an "exercise" price. For example, Moody's KMV estimates default probabilities using this approach, with proprietary adjustments to the input variables, such as the face value of debt. The CreditGrades model, developed jointly by Deutsche Bank, Goldman Sachs, JP Morgan, and RiskMetrics, introduces an uncertain default point, which arguably is more realistic than the use of certain default points. Figure 6.9 illustrates this.

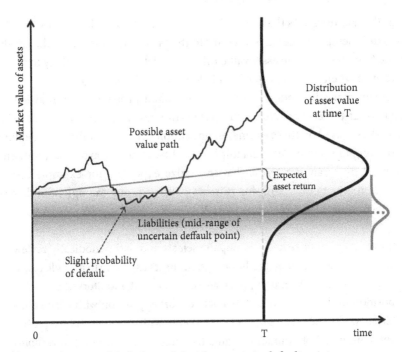

Figure 6.9 Structural default model with uncertain default point

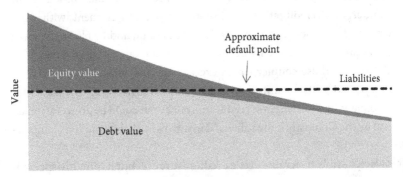

Figure 6.10 Debt and equity values when total assets fall below liabilities

A word of caution: the structural models imply that default occurs when the market value dips below the firm's liabilities, and that the probability of default can be estimated as the probability that the market value dips below the liabilities. But this is not the same as the probability that the equity value will fall to zero! I have seen an expert witness make this erroneous assumption in a major lawsuit, which led to some deeply flawed conclusions. Figure 6.10 illustrates this point. With a high asset value, the debt value is close to the principal value (i.e., the liabilities). As the asset value falls, the debt value (but not the liabilities) declines and trades at a discount to the principal value. Thus, the equity value (which equals the asset value minus the debt value) is unlikely to reach zero even when the asset value is far below the firm's liabilities.

In summary, it is possible to estimate default probability from available data about the companies or purchase estimates from several commercial providers. Based on these estimates, one should tread carefully when dealing with companies with high default probability, either by avoiding them entirely or by arranging terms that minimize exposure, for example, using shorter maturity or asking for suitable collateral. For example, Southwest Airlines reported the following in its 2016 10K:

> To manage credit risk, the Company selects and will periodically review counterparties based on credit ratings, limits its exposure to a single counterparty with collateral support agreements, and monitors the market position of the program and its relative market position with each counterparty. . . . the Company had agreements with all of its counterparties containing early termination rights triggered by credit rating thresholds and/or bilateral collateral provisions whereby security is required if market risk exposure exceeds a specified threshold amount based on the counterparty's credit rating. The Company also had agreements with counterparties in which cash deposits, letters of credit, and/or pledged aircraft are required to be posted whenever the net fair value of derivatives associated with those counterparties exceeds specific thresholds—cash is either posted by the counterparty if the value of derivatives is an asset to the Company, or cash, letters of credit, and/or aircraft could be posted as collateral by the Company if the value of derivatives is a liability to the Company.

It is also possible to acquire trade credit insurance, but it is highly specialized and not always available.

6.6 Credit Default Swaps (CDSs)

A Credit Default Swap (CDS) is essentially an insurance contract in which the "buyer" makes a series of payments to the "seller" in exchange for a payoff if the underlying loan defaults. Thus, CDSs are suitable for mitigating credit risk and risk from investing in bonds.

Interestingly, CDSs can also be used for speculative purposes. Because the regulators do not recognize CDSs as insurance (perhaps due to their deceptive name?), they are not regulated as such and can be bought and sold by just about anybody. That is, you can acquire CDSs even if you do not own the underlying bonds. So, if you believe that Argentina will default on its bonds, you can place a bet on that belief by purchasing CDSs on the country's bonds. In contrast, only parties with an *insurable interest* can purchase regulated insurance products. For example, you can buy life insurance on yourself or your spouse, but not on strangers, which, as you can imagine, would create perverse incentives.[3]

The annual payments on a CDS constitute the spread, and the spread is expressed as a fraction of the notional amount. For example, if a CDS spread is 80 basis points, or 0.80%, a buyer of $1 million worth of insurance protection must pay $8,000 annually, which is typically broken up in quarterly payments of $2,000.

Consider the example in Figure 6.11. The buyer of the CDS pays the spread of 350 basis points each year, and the bond defaults in the fourth year. As a result, the buyer of the CDS is entitled to 80% of par, provided that the company only pays 20% (the recovery rate) of its obligation. Notice that this is essentially the same example as the earlier insurance example, except that I replaced the factory with bonds and there is no deductible. I did this on purpose to illustrate the similarity of CDSs to conventional insurance.

The spread primarily depends on the probability of default and the recovery rate (the fraction of notional repaid in event of default). Thus, if the spread and the recovery rate are known, the probability of default can be inferred, which means that CDS spreads can be used to gauge creditworthiness.

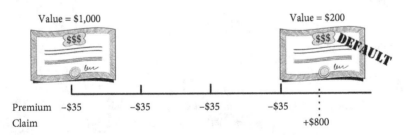

Figure 6.11 Example of Credit Default Swap (CDS)

---

[3] And, yes, the police and insurance companies are very much aware of the mixed incentive when you get life insurance on your spouse, a popular backdrop in crime books and movies.

Let us simplify with a one-year contract. Suppose that the underlying bond pays $100 if it does not default, but only $20 if it defaults, so that the recovery rate is 20%. Further, suppose that the probability of default, p, is 10%. What would you pay for insurance that guarantees a $100 payment? There is a 10% chance that the insurance would pay $80 (to make you whole if the bond only pays $20), so a fair price would be $p \times \$80 = 10\% \times \$80 = \$8$, which implies a spread of $8 / $100 = 8%. We can reverse this to express the default probability as:

$$p = \frac{\$8}{\$80} = \frac{CDS\ spread \times \$100}{\left(1 - recovery\ rate\right) \times \$100} = \frac{CDS\ spread}{1 - recovery\ rate}$$

Now, let us examine the fascinating example of Lehman Brothers before and during the financial crisis. The creditworthiness of Lehman Brothers was very important to both its creditors and the many companies and individuals that had entered various types of financial contracts with Lehman Brothers. Figure 6.12 shows the one-year and five-year CDS spreads on Lehman Brothers bonds in the two years leading up to its bankruptcy filing on Monday, September 15, 2008. It also displays the stock price for comparison. The one-year spread provides information on the default probability during the next year, whereas the five-year spread provides information on the annualized default probability during the next five years. The average one-year spread from January 2005 through June 2007 was 9 points. The

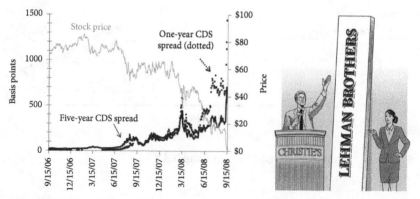

Figure 6.12 The CDS spread for Lehman Brothers

one-year spread on Friday, September 12, 2008, when default was imminent, was 1,443 points.

Suppose that the recovery rate was expected to be about 30%. This is roughly in line with historical defaults in the financial sector. Based on the one-year spread of 9 points, the implied default probability was only 0.09% / (1 − 30%) = 0.1%. But based on the one-year spread of about 700 points during the couple of months before the bankruptcy filing, the implied default probability was 7% / (1 − 30%) = 10%, and this roughly doubled to 20% on September 12, 2008. The irony here is that we use CDSs (in this case on Lehman bonds) to gauge the default probability of a company whose downfall was, in large part, due to the unregulated market of CDSs (on mortgage bonds).

While the dramatic increase in default probability is consistent with actual events, it is puzzling that the spread was not higher yet when bankruptcy was seemingly inevitable during the second week of September 2008. Perhaps this points to the difficulty of predicting default, even when you are looking straight at it. It is also interesting to note that the five-year spread was significantly lower than the one-year spread during the month before the bankruptcy filing. Because the five-year rate can be viewed as a weighted average of the one-year rate and the rate from year 2 through year 5, this can interpreted as the market estimating the default probability to be much higher in year 1 than in the subsequent four years. That is, if Lehman could only survive the next year, it would be on safer ground.

7

Hedging with Forward and Futures Contracts

7.1 Forward and futures contracts

Both *forward* and *futures contracts* call for future delivery of a certain commodity at a price specified today. They allow us to enter contracts to either buy a commodity in the future (also called buying forwards/futures or "going long" forwards/futures) or sell a commodity in the future (also called selling forwards/futures or "going short" forwards/futures) at a fixed price.

Forward contracts only involve two parties, and, as such, can be tailor-made to fit the needs of the parties. They do, however, have a couple of disadvantages:

(a) Default risk is high—if the counterparty is unable to fulfill the obligations, you will be at a loss. Consequently, forward contracts are available only to creditworthy customers.
(b) The contracts are illiquid—it might be difficult to find a counterparty for a contract, and it is difficult to cancel a contract.

Unlike forward contracts, *futures contracts* are standardized with regard to the size of the contract, delivery date, etc., and trade on an organized exchange. As a result, futures contracts have the following:

(a) High liquidity—To enter or cancel a contract, you can simply contact your broker, who, in turn, will trade contracts on the exchange.
(b) Low default risk—The exchange clearinghouse guarantees both sides of the contract, thereby reducing default risk to a minimum.

There are a couple of consequences of these features. First, to minimize its risk as the guarantor, the exchange imposes margin requirements and settles profits and losses daily. For example, if you suffer a large paper loss on a

Applied Corporate Risk and Liquidity Management. Erik Lie, Oxford University Press. © Oxford University Press 2023.
DOI: 10.1093/oso/9780197664995.003.0007

contract one day, you might have to deposit more money with your broker to cover those losses.[1] Second, because the contracts are not tailor-made, users of contracts for hedging purposes are more likely to cancel the contracts immediately before expiration. For example, a corn farmer might dislike the delivery location or the maximum moisture content specified in the forward contract and, therefore, prefers to deliver elsewhere.

7.2 Forward/futures prices versus spot prices

Forward prices (or futures prices), current spot prices, and expected future spot prices are all naturally linked, and it is imperative for users of forward and futures contracts to understand these relations. There are prominent examples of how failure to either understand these relations or to capture them in the estimation of profits have had devastating effects. For example, in the early 1990s, Kidder, Peabody & Co.'s accounting system recorded a purchase of a commodity at a spot price and a simultaneous sale of the same commodity at a higher forward price as an instantaneous profit. One of its traders, Joseph Jett, took advantage of this flaw via trades over several years, thus accumulating large paper profits, while in reality the trades led to actual losses of $350 million.

Figure 7.1 shows the relations between forward prices, current spot prices, and expected future spot prices. Let us first consider the relation between forward prices, F_0, and spot prices, S_0, which we will formalize as the *cost-of-carry relationship*.

We can obtain an asset at some future date by either (i) purchasing the asset now and storing it until the future date, or (ii) taking a long position in a forward (or futures) contract on the asset and accepting delivery on the future date. Because the end result is the same, the cost should also be the same. Thus, there should be some relationship between the current cost of the asset, the holding cost, and the futures price of the asset.

Suppose that we wish to acquire a stock at some future date T. We can buy the stock today at price S_0 and hold it until time T, at which time the price will be S_T. Alternatively, we can initiate a long futures position, and invest sufficient money today to pay the futures price when the contract matures at time

---

[1] In fact, you are given a new contract every day with a new price that reflects the new market price, as if you sold the old contract and bought a new one.

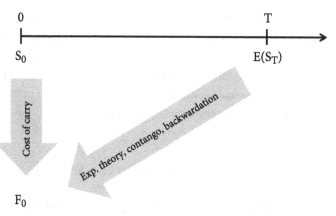

Figure 7.1 The relations between forward and spot prices

T. Hence, the necessary investment today equals $F_0 / (1 + r_f)^T$, where F_0 is the futures price today and r_f is the risk-free rate. Because these alternatives give the same outcome at time T, the costs should be the same, that is,

$$S_0 = \frac{F_0}{(1+r_f)^T} \Leftrightarrow F_0 = S_0(1+r_f)^T$$

If we also include a dividend yield of d, we get:

$$F_0 = S_0(1+r_f - d)^T$$

There might also be costs (other than interest) of carrying commodities from today to time T, including storage costs, insurance costs, and the allowance for spoilage of goods in storage. Offsetting these costs, there might be some convenience/benefit of holding the commodity (e.g., the dividend in the stock example, the utility of holding gold as jewelry, or the operational flexibility of keeping an oil inventory). If we define c to be the net of these costs and benefits in percentage terms, we get a general expression for the *spot-futures parity theorem* or *cost-of-carry relationship*:

$$F_0 = S_0(1+r_f + c)^T$$

Incidentally, in the special case of currencies where there are two risk-free interest rates, the spot-futures relationship turns into the *interest rate parity*:

$$F_0 = S_0 \left(\frac{1 + r_{home}}{1 + r_{foreign}} \right)^T$$

where both S_0 and F_0 are given as *direct* exchange rates (i.e., the home currency cost of one foreign currency unit), r_{home} is the risk-free rate at home, and $r_{foreign}$ is the risk-free rate in the foreign country.

Now, let's turn to the relation between forward prices and expected future spot prices. There are three general possibilities:

1. *Expectations hypothesis*: $F_0 = E(S_T)$. The expectations hypothesis simply states that the forward rate is an unbiased forecast of the future spot price. That is, with a large enough sample of forward prices and later spot prices on the contract expiration dates, the averages of the two sets of prices are the same.

2. *Backwardation*: $F_0 < E(S_T)$. Backwardation implies that the spot price on the expiration of a forward contract tends to be higher than the forward price. There are a couple of possible reasons for this:

   i. <u>Systematic risk</u>: The underlying asset has *positive* systematic risk (ß>0), for which investors holding the futures contracts require compensation.

   ii. <u>Demand/supply imbalance</u>: If hedgers typically want to keep short positions (like farmers), they will have to compensate some speculators to take long positions. This requires the futures price to be less than the expected spot price ($F_0 < E(S_T)$) so that the expected profit to the long position is positive ($E(S_T) - F_0 > 0$).

3. *Contango*: $F_0 > E(S_T)$. Contango implies that the spot price on the expiration of a forward contract tends to be lower than the forward price. There are a couple of possible reasons for this:

   i. <u>Systematic risk</u>: The underlying asset has *negative* systematic risk (ß<0).

   ii. <u>Demand/supply imbalance</u>: If hedgers typically want to keep long positions (like grain processors), they will have to compensate some speculators to take short positions. This requires the futures price to be higher than the expected spot price ($F_0 > E(S_T)$) so that the expected profit to the short position is positive ($F_0 - E(S_T) > 0$).

Before we proceed, I want to mention a caveat. I have defined *backwardation* as $F_0 < E(S_T)$, but it is sometimes used to refer to $F_0 < S_0$. Similarly, I have defined *contango* as $F_0 > E(S_T)$, but it is sometimes used to refer to $F_0 > S_0$. This, unfortunately, can cause some confusion when you read the financial press.

Figure 7.2 shows the typical patterns for forward prices relative to future spot prices for the three theories. Gold (which has low, and perhaps even negative, systematic risk) is pictured as an example of contango, while oil (with positive systematic risk) is pictured as an example of backwardation.

The stock example from Figure 7.3 shows how all relations fit together. Suppose the risk-free rate is 3% and the market risk premium is 7%. Based

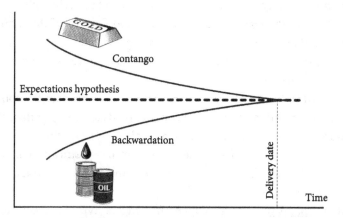

Figure 7.2 Contango, backwardation, and the expectations hypothesis

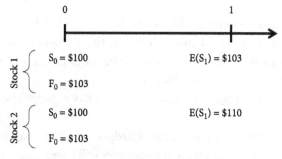

Figure 7.3 Stock example

on the CAPM, we can calculate expected returns for two stocks with no dividends:

- Stock 1: Beta = 0 (thus, no systematic risk) → Expected return = 3%
- Stock 2: Beta = 1 (positive systematic risk) → Expected return = 10%

If both stocks are currently priced at $100, the first is expected to increase to $103 in a year, while the second is expected to increase to $110. Furthermore, the cost-of-carry relation implies that the price for one-year forward contracts on either stock is:

$$F_0 = S_0(1 + r_f - d)^T = \$100(1 + 3\% - 0\%)^1 = \$103$$

Thus, we see that $F_0 = E(S_T)$ for the stock with no systematic risk, and $F_0 < E(S_T)$, implying backwardation, for the stock with positive systematic risk. In theory, we would get contango if Beta < 0.

7.3 A spectacular example: Oil prices during the COVID-19 pandemic

Figure 7.4 shows that on April 20, 2020, the spot price for WTI oil fell into negative territory, meaning that producers of oil would pay customers to take it off their hands. This was the result of a slump in demand and full storage facilities. But the futures prices remained in a more reasonable territory. For example, the spot price closed at –$37 per barrel on April 20, while the price for oil with delivery in August closed at $29 per barrel on the same day. With rock-bottom interest rates (the six-month Treasury rate was 0.15%), it was essentially possible to make a profit if you could buy at –$37 and sell at $29 and the storage cost was lower than $66 per barrel.

A *Wall Street Journal* titled "Oil Buyers Try Out Crude Storage Ideas" dated May 12, 2020, described the rush to identify reasonable storage alternatives, including two pals from Texas who rented hundreds of bus-size metal tanks and filled them with some 300,000 barrels of oil, water companies that stored crude oil in cylinders resembling above-ground swimming pools, and a

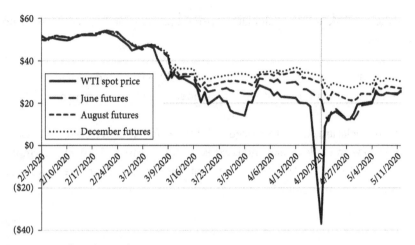

Figure 7.4 The oil price becomes negative

mining company that looked into converting abandoned mines to hold millions of barrels of crude oil (but, fortunately, regulators balked).

7.4 Basis risk

As noted earlier, futures contracts cannot be tailored with regard to contract size, maturity, commodity, etc., to meet the unique needs of each hedger. As a result, hedges based on futures contracts are imperfect. For example, Southwest Airlines reported the following in its 2016 10K:

> A portion of the fuel derivatives in the Company's hedge portfolio are based on the market price of West Texas intermediate crude oil ("WTI"). In recent years, jet fuel prices have been more closely correlated with changes in the price of Brent crude oil ("Brent"). The Company has attempted to mitigate some of this risk by entering into more fuel hedges based on Brent crude. . . . Jet fuel is not widely traded on an organized futures exchange and, therefore, there are limited opportunities to hedge directly in jet fuel for time horizons longer than approximately 24 months into the future.

These imperfect hedges give rise to basis risk. The *basis* is defined as:

$$b = \text{Spot price of asset to be hedged } (S) - \text{Futures price of contract used} (F)$$

The spot and futures prices can refer to identical or similar underlying assets. If the assets are indeed identical, we can rearrange the cost-of-carry relationship to get some insight about the determinants of the basis:

$$F_0 = S_0(1+r_f+c)^T \Rightarrow \frac{S_0}{F_0} = \frac{1}{(1+r_f+c)^T}$$

That means that, if the spot and futures prices refer to identical assets, then

- the basis < 0 if $r_f + c > 0$,
- the basis approaches 0 as T approaches 0, and
- changes in either storage costs or convenience yield could trigger changes in the basis.

Ok—it is time for an example. Suppose that we have a long asset position (e.g., we own a stock), and we would like to hedge by entering a short futures position at time $t = 1$ and exit at time $t = 2$ when we intend to sell the asset. However, the futures contract does not expire at $t = 2$, but rather at some point afterward. Consequently, we will be exposed to *basis risk*, that is, risk associated with an uncertain basis at $t = 2$. This is shown in Figure 7.5.

- At $t = 1$: $S_1 = \$25$ and $F_1 = \$22$, such that $b_1 = \$25 - \$22 = \$3$. Incidentally, because the basis is positive, there must be a convenience yield on the asset, such as a dividend.
- At $t = 2$: $S_2 = \$20$ and $F_2 = \$19$, such that $b_2 = \$20 - \$19 = \$1$. As expected, the basis has narrowed as expiration approaches. But we don't know exactly what b_2 is until $t = 2$.

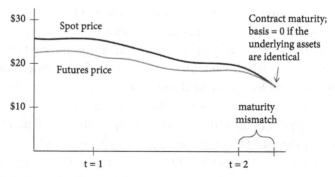

Figure 7.5 Example of basis risk

At $t = 2$, we sell the asset for S_2, and realize the profit on futures position $F_1 - F_2$, giving a total hedged inflow of $S_2 + F_1 - F_2 = F_1 + b_2$. Had b_2 been known at time $t = 1$, we would have had a perfect hedge. This is the case if the futures contract expires at $t = 2$ *and* the asset underlying the futures contract is identical to the asset to be sold (in which case $b_2 = 0$). But in this case, the futures contract expires after $t = 2$, so the hedge comes with some basis risk.

Suppose now that the asset to be sold differs from the asset underlying the futures contract (e.g., we use an S&P futures contract to hedge a stock position), and S^* denotes the spot price of the asset underlying the futures contract. Then the total hedged inflow at $t = 2$ can be written as:

$$S_2 + F_1 - F_2 = F_1 + (S_2^* - F_2) + (S_2 - S_2^*)$$

where $(S_2^* - F_2)$ is the basis arising from the difference between $t = 2$ and contract maturity, and $(S_2 - S_2^*)$ is the basis arising from the difference in assets.

This shows that, to minimize basis risk, we should choose (i) a delivery month for the futures contract that is as close as possible to the expiration of the hedge, and (2) an asset underlying the futures contract with high price correlation with the asset to be hedged. The next section on cross-hedging considers the second issue further.

7.5 Cross-hedging

Cross-hedging occurs when the asset underlying the futures contract differs from the asset whose price is being hedged. Examples include investors using futures contract on the S&P 500 to hedge diversified stock positions that resemble the behavior and performance of the overall market portfolio, or airlines using futures contract on crude oil to hedge jet fuel costs. I will cover a detailed example of the latter after covering some technicalities.

One issue with cross-hedging is that the volatility of the asset in our unhedged position might differ from the volatility of the futures contracts. Suppose, for example, that we hold a diversified portfolio of stocks with an average beta of 1.5 that we seek to hedge by shorting a futures contract on the S&P 500 index. Because the volatility of our position is 1.5 times higher than that on the S&P 500 index, we must compensate by adjusting up the number of futures contracts we need for this purpose. That brings us to the hedge ratio.

The *hedge ratio* (*H*) is the ratio of the size of the position in futures contracts to the size of the exposure. The change in the value of a hedged position can then be written as $\Delta S - H\Delta F$, and the variance of the change is:

$$\sigma_{\Delta S}^2 - H^2 \sigma_{\Delta F}^2 - 2H\rho\sigma_{\Delta S}\sigma_{\Delta F}$$

We generally seek to minimize this variance by selecting the hedge ratio. It can be shown that the *Minimum Variance Hedge Ratio* (*H**) is

$$H^* = \rho\frac{\sigma_{\Delta S}}{\sigma_{\Delta F}}$$

which can be found as the slope of a regression of ΔS against ΔF. Thus, if the correlation is one, the optimal hedge ratio equals the relative standard deviation of the spot contract to the futures contract. For example, if the spot contract is twice as volatile as the futures contract, the optimal hedge ratio equals 2 to compensate for the low volatility of the futures contract. Moreover, the equation shows that as the correlation decreases and the hedge becomes less effective, the optimal hedge ratio also decreases.

If we then plug *H** in for *H* in the variance equation, we get the variance of the minimum variance hedged position:

$$\sigma_{\Delta S}^2 - \rho^2\sigma_{\Delta S}^2 = (1-\rho^2)\sigma_{\Delta S}^2$$

The corresponding standard deviation is simply

$$\sqrt{1-\rho^2} \times \sigma_{\Delta S}$$

and the fraction of the standard deviation $\sigma_{\Delta S}$ that can be reduced via cross-hedging is

$$100\% - \sqrt{1-\rho^2}$$

which is illustrated in Figure 7.6.

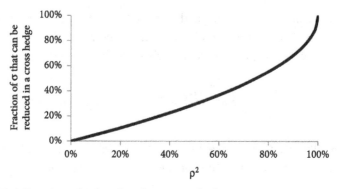

Figure 7.6 Fraction of risk reduced in a cross hedge

This shows that a higher absolute value for the correlation ρ yields a better hedge. Thus, cross-hedging works even if the correlation is *negative*. But then the cross hedge entails taking a hedged position in the *same* direction as the original position, that is, a long-hedged position for a long original position, and a short-hedged position for a short original position, just as if were diversifying a portfolio.

Now let us proceed with a practical example. It is June 2020, and an airline expects to purchase 2.1 million gallons (50,000 barrels) of jet fuel in a little less than four months. Given the currently low jet fuel prices and the struggling operations of the airline during the COVID-19 pandemic, the airline seeks to lock in the price. Because no four-month jet fuel futures contracts are available, the airline decides to buy four-month WTI crude oil futures to hedge its price exposure.[2] Other assumptions follow:

- One crude oil futures contract involves 1,000 barrels.
- Prices:
  - o Spot price for jet fuel: $39.40 per barrel
  - o Spot price for crude oil: $38.17 per barrel
  - o Four-month crude oil futures price: $38.80 per barrel

---

[2] Trading in the WTI futures contracts ends three business days prior to the 25th calendar day of the month prior to the contract month. Because we intend to use the WTI futures contract to hedge by taking any profit or loss from the trading of the futures contract to offset the price movements in the jet fuel spot market (i.e., we do not actually want to take delivery of the crude oil), we need to get out of the contract *before* the contract month. Thus, it might make more sense to use a five-month WTI futures contract in this example, depending on exactly when we need to purchase the jet fuel.

Incidentally, that means that the annualized net cost of carrying oil over the next four months (based on the cost-of-carry relation) given a risk-free rate of 0.2% is:

$$\$38.80 = \$38.17(1 + 0.2\% + c)^{4/12} \Rightarrow c = 4.8\%$$

meaning that storage costs exceed the convenience of carrying oil.

The main questions we will answer are the following:

- How many contracts should the airline buy?
- And how much would the risk decline?

Figure 7.7 shows the time series of jet fuel spot prices and crude oil futures prices. It is evident that there is substantial positive correlation, and the use of crude oil futures should provide a reasonable hedge.

Figure 7.8 shows a scatter plot of the jet fuel spot returns versus the crude oil futures returns, along with a regression line. The *Minimum Variance Hedge Ratio* (H^*) is 0.86 and ρ^2 is 0.50.

Fifty thousand barrels of jet fuel have a value of $50,000 \times \$39.40 = \$1,970,000$. Thus, a naïve hedge using four-month crude oil futures contracts involves contracts with a value of $1,970,000. But because jet fuel prices only change by about 86% of any change in the crude oil futures prices, such a naïve hedge would end up being "too much."

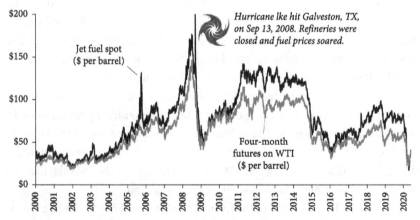

Figure 7.7 Jet fuel spot prices and crude oil futures prices

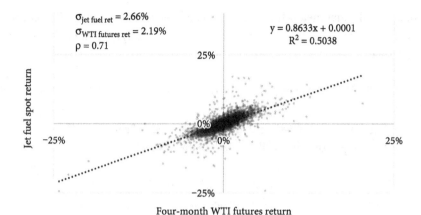

$\sigma_{\text{jet fuel ret}} = 2.66\%$
$\sigma_{\text{WTI futures ret}} = 2.19\%$
$\rho = 0.71$

$y = 0.8633x + 0.0001$
$R^2 = 0.5038$

Figure 7.8 Scatter plot of jet fuel spot returns vs. crude oil futures returns

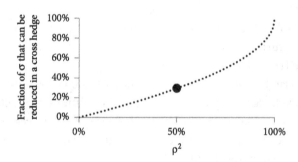

Figure 7.9 Fraction of risk reduced in the airline example

Using the minimum variance hedge ratio, the adjusted value of the four-month crude oil futures contracts is $1.97 million × 0.863 = $1.7 million, which is the equivalent of $1.7 million / $38.80 = 43,814 barrels ≈ 44 futures contracts. This hedge should reduce the standard deviation by $100\% - \sqrt{1 - 0.5038} = 30\%$, as illustrated in Figure 7.9.

Let us see how this hedge works. If the crude oil increases by 10% in the futures market, then this is expected to be accompanied by an increase in the jet fuel price of 8.63%. The airline's jet fuel costs are expected to increase by 8.63% × $1,970,000 = $170,000, whereas the futures contracts increase in value by 10% × 44 × 1,000 × $38.30 = $171,000. In other words, the two values are almost perfectly balanced, as shown in Figure 7.10.

However, a 10% increase in the futures market for oil might not be accompanied by an 8.63% increase in the jet fuel market as expected. It might very

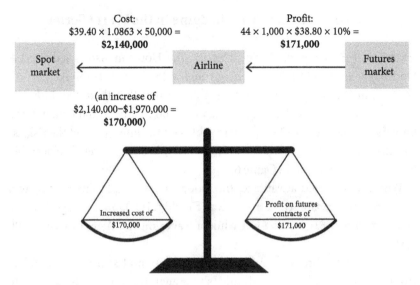

Figure 7.10 Perfectly balanced hedge

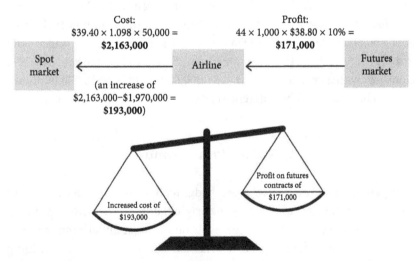

Figure 7.11 Imperfectly balanced hedge

well be that the jet fuel price increases, say, 9.8% instead. If so, the hedge works less effectively, as the profit from the futures contract of $171,000 only covers part of the increased cost of 9.8% × $1,970,000 = $193,000. This is shown in Figure 7.11.

7.6 An example: Cross-hedging in the World Series

After Game 5 of the 2017 World Series, the Houston Astros led the LA Dodgers 3–2. Ticket brokers owning roughly 15,000 tickets for each World Series game at Dodgers Stadium were concerned that there would be no Game 7. At an expected average price of $2,000 in a potential Game 7, the brokers had more than $20 million in profits on the line. To offset the risk associated with the ticket sales for Game 7, many brokers therefore placed big bets on Houston to win in Game 6.

With a home-field advantage, the Dodgers were slight favorites to win Game 6 (the probability of a win was roughly 51%), and a wager on the Dodgers to win $100 cost $114 while a wager on the Astros to win $100 cost $105.

Suppose that a broker would make an incremental $1 million in profits from Game 7. How much should she wager in Game 6 to eliminate the risk?

If the broker places a wager on the Astros in the amount of $105 × x, the broker will get $100 × x if the Astros win and $1,000,000 − $105 × x if they lose. The value for x that equates these, and, thus, eliminates the risk, is $1,000,000 / 205 = 4,878$, meaning that the broker should wager $105 × 4,878 = $512,190$. The guaranteed payoff of $100 × 4,878 = $487,800$ compares with an expected profit of $1,000,000 × 51% = $510,000$ in the absence of hedging, and the difference of $22,200 is the bookmaker's cut.

7.7 Rolling futures contracts

Companies sometimes use cross-hedging because long-term futures contracts on the asset underlying the original unhedged position are unavailable. However, short-term contracts on the asset underlying the original position are often available. Thus, an alternative to cross-hedging is to roll over short-term contracts on the asset underlying the original position.

Suppose an airline needs to buy one million gallons of jet fuel at some distant point into the future, say in one year. If the airline could enter one-year futures contracts to hedge this purchase, it would be perfectly hedged. An alternative is to enter a six-month futures contract now, and then enter a second six-month futures contract when the first has expired. However,

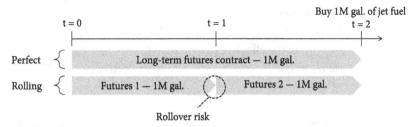

Figure 7.12 Rolling futures contracts and rollover risk

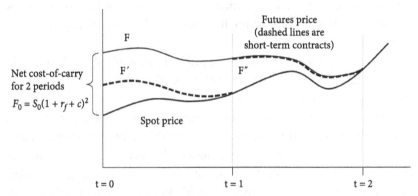

Figure 7.13 Long-term vs. rolling hedge

this alternative comes with *rollover risk*, that is, risk that the basis has moved in the airline's disfavor when the futures contract is renewed. Figure 7.12 illustrates this.

Let us look more closely at this risk based on Figure 7.13. In this case, the hedger (the airline) is **short** the asset (jet fuel) and needs to buy at $t = 2$. The two alternative hedging strategies are:

- Long-term hedge: Take a <u>long-term</u> **long** futures position at $t = 0$.
  - o Realized price $= -S_2$ (negative to indicate a cost)
  - o Profit on futures position $= F_2 - F_0$
  - o Effective price $= -S_2 + F_2 - F_0 = -F_0 - b_2$
  - o Because $b_2 = 0$, the effective price $= -F_0$ (negative to indicate a cost)
- Rolling hedge: Take a <u>short-term</u> **long** futures position at $t = 0$ and roll it over at $t = 1$.
  - o Realized price $= -S_2$
  - o Profit on futures position $1 = F'_1 - F'_0$

- o Profit on futures position 2 = $F''_2 - F''_1$
- o Effective price = $-S_2 + F'_1 - F'_0 + F''_2 - F''_1 = F'_1 - F'_0 - F''_1 - b''_2$
- o Because $b''_2 = 0$, the effective price = $F'_1 - F'_0 - F''_1$
- o Because $b'_1 = S_1 - F'_1 = 0$, $S_1 = F'_1$ and the effective price = $S_1 - F'_0 - F''_1 = -F'_0 + b''_1$

Thus, the long-term hedge comes with no risk, while the rolling hedge has some rollover risk from the uncertainty of what the basis of the second contract will be at $t = 1$. In most cases, this risk is modest.

Consider a couple of scenarios illustrated in Figure 7.14. In both scenarios, the long-term futures contract implies a price of $-F_0 = -\$3.10$ (negative to indicate a cost).

The rolling contracts implies a net price of $-F'_0 + b''_1 = -\$3.05 + b''_1$. In the first scenario, $b''_1 = -\$0.06$ (which is similar to $b'_1 = -\$0.05$), making the net price $-\$3.05 - \$0.06 = -\$3.11$. Obviously, had $b'_1 = b''_1$ (meaning no change in the short-term basis), the net price would have been the same as when using a long-term futures contract. In the second scenario, a hurricane shuts down refineries shortly before $t = 1$, thereby increasing the convenience of holding jet fuel that is temporarily in short supply, decreasing the net carrying cost c, and increasing b''_1 to $+\$0.08$. As a result, the net price is $-\$3.05 + \$0.08 = -\$2.97$. This illustrates that the rollover risk arises from shocks to the net carrying cost c (or, alternatively, shocks to the interest rate r_f).

Incidentally, if the hedger instead starts with a long position that she wants to sell at $t = 2$, the long-term hedge yields an effective price of F_0, while the rolling hedge gives an effective price of $F'_0 - b''_1$. Thus, the effective price of the rolling hedge again depends on the uncertain basis for the second futures contract at $t = 1$.

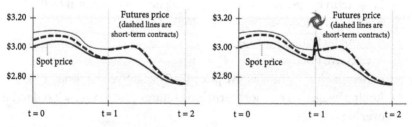

Figure 7.14 Alternative scenarios

7.8 More on hedging long-term exposure

Most companies have risk exposure that extends several years into the future. For example, an airline will not only have to buy jet fuel over the next year, but also the years thereafter (until a new energy source emerges or airplanes go obsolete). In reality, firms often hedge for the shorter-term, for example, for the next year or two at a time. And firms that hedge, say one year at a time, might still claim to be 100% hedged.

What is the consequence of an airline hedging the jet fuel consumption for only one period at a time? Figure 7.15 illustrates an airline that needs jet fuel for each of the next two periods.

i. A perfect hedge entails using a one-period contract to hedge the jet fuel consumption for the next period and a two-period contract to hedge the jet fuel consumption for the second period.

ii. If two-period contracts are unavailable, the airline can use a rolling hedge for the consumption for the second period, in which case the airline is exposed to rollover risk.

iii. As a third alternative, the airline can enter a one-period contract now to hedge the consumption for the first period, and then wait until the beginning of the second period to enter another one-period contract to hedge the consumption for the second period. As the diagram shows, this implies that the cost of the second-period consumption is left exposed during the first period.

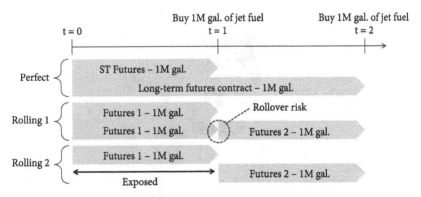

Figure 7.15 Hedging over two periods

A later simulation example shows that the third hedging strategy, while per-haps the most common strategy to hedge long-term risk, is less effective than the other two strategies.

7.9 The collateral dilemma

Entering derivative contracts often requires collateral to cover future payments to counterparties. For example, Southwest Airlines 2016 10K shows that its hedging activities required both cash and aircrafts as collateral:

> The gross fair value of outstanding financial derivative instruments related to the Company's jet fuel market price risk at December 31, 2015, was a net lia-bility of $1.5 billion. In addition, $835 million in cash collateral deposits and $250 million in aircraft collateral were provided by the Company in connec-tion with these instruments based on their fair value as of December 31, 2015.

Thus, firms might face a dilemma in whether to collateralize their assets for derivative hedging or for debt, as illustrated in Figure 7.16. If a firm ties up assets as collateral in its hedging, it might lose its financial flexibility to raise debt that requires collateral. If it instead ties up assets as debt collateral, it might not be able to hedge.

Derivative   Debt
collateral?   collateral?

Figure 7.16 The collateral dilemma

The dilemma could have severe consequences for firms in financial distress. Risk management theory predicts that firms that are closest to financial distress benefit the most from hedging. On that basis, one would expect that these firms engage in more hedging. However, financially distressed firms might lack assets that are not already collateralized, and if they still have some collateralization capacity, they might need that for debt issues. Thus, distressed firms are effectively shut out of the derivatives market.

8

Hedging with Options

8.1 Options and option prices

An option gives the holder the right, *but not the obligation,* to buy or sell an asset for a specified price X (*exercise or strike price*) on or before some specified *expiration date*. A *call* option gives the right to *buy*, whereas a *put* option gives the right to *sell*.

It sounds great to be the holder of such options, right? As an option holder, you have the flexibility to do something (i.e., buy or sell an asset such as a stock) if it suits you, but you do not have to do anything. Well, that flexibility has a price, and that price must be paid when you buy the options. The prices of the options, called *option premiums*, are generally denoted C for call options and P for put options.[1]

Let us pause here for a minute. We have already introduced several prices, and students easily get confused. To be clear, when you buy an option, you must pay the option premium, whereas the seller of an option naturally receives the premium instead. And if you as the option holder choose to exercise your right to buy or sell the underlying asset, the transaction price will be the exercise price, X, which is clearly specified in the option contract and does not change. Furthermore, there are usually many different option contracts available with different exercises prices, and they all come with different premiums depending on the exercise prices and other information.

As an aside, if you enter a <u>forward</u> (or futures) contracts, there is no upfront premium to be paid. Furthermore, you cannot choose the future transaction price from an array of alternatives; there is only one future transaction price available, the forward price F, and it is dictated by the market.

---

[1] In this case, the word "premium" is used in place of "price." Incidentally, that is also the case in the world of insurance, where insurance premium describes the price of the insurance product. But in other places of this book, premium is used to describe how one price relates to another. For example, a forward premium (as opposed to a forward discount) indicates that the forward price exceeds the spot price.

Applied Corporate Risk and Liquidity Management. Erik Lie, Oxford University Press. © Oxford University Press 2023.
DOI: 10.1093/oso/9780197664995.003.0008

8.2 Option value components

Option values (i.e., option premiums) can be decomposed into two components:

(1) The *intrinsic value* is the value of the option if it is immediately exercised (or, alternatively, the value at expiration). A call option has no intrinsic value if the stock price is below the exercise price (because the option holder will choose not to exercise), in which case we refer to the option as being "out-of-the-money." But as the stock price exceeds the exercise price and gets "in-the-money," the intrinsic value equals the differences between the two prices. Conversely, a put option has no intrinsic value if the stock price exceeds the exercise price (because the option holder will choose not to exercise), in which case we refer to the option as being "out-of-the-money." But as the stock price falls below the exercise price and gets "in-the-money," the intrinsic value equals the differences between the two prices. In short, we can write the intrinsic values for call and put options in the following way:

- Call option: $Max[S - X, 0]$
- Put option: $Max[X - S, 0]$

where S is the stock price and X is the exercise price.

(2) The *time value* is whatever market value an option currently has above its intrinsic value. Regardless of whether the options are in-the-money or out-of-the-money, they have some time value. For example, if the stock price is currently below the exercise price, a call option has no intrinsic value, yet the option must have some value as long as there is some chance for the stock price to increase beyond the exercise price by the maturity date. The chance that this occurs increases with <u>time</u> until maturity and the <u>volatility</u> of the stock price. That is why we refer to this additional value as <u>time value</u>.[2]

Figure 8.1 shows the two values for call and put options. Most of this chapter focuses on the intrinsic value because we generally hold options used for hedging until maturity when the time value has evaporated. But it is also

---

[2] A more fitting name would be <u>time × volatility value</u>, but that just isn't very catchy. Recall that if we have the volatility measured by standard deviation for one period, we can estimate the volatility for several periods by multiplying by the square root of the number of periods: $\sigma \times \sqrt{T}$. This is the term that shows up in the Black-Scholes valuation formula to capture the time value.

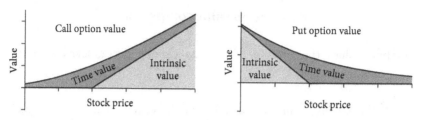

Figure 8.1 The values of call and put options

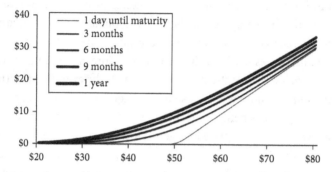

Figure 8.2 The declining time value for a call option

useful to be able to estimate the total value, including when we use delta hedging later in this chapter.

Figure 8.2 illustrates how the time value evaporates over time for a call option as we approach maturity, until we basically only have the intrinsic value left. Thus, we often interchange the terms intrinsic value and value at expiration.

It is beyond the scope of this book to derive the value of options. I will not even provide any option valuation formulas here. Rather, I will simply refer to the option valuation calculators that you can easily look up on the internet. One thing that is handy to know in our context, however, is how to deal with the net cost-of-carry (storage costs less the benefits of holding the underlying commodity). You will see that most option valuation calculators based on the Black-Scholes valuation formula allow you to insert a dividend, which is one of the benefits of holding a security. Thus, to estimate the value of an option on a commodity, we can simply insert that net cost-of-carry as a negative dividend.

Consider an example of options on coffee beans. The spot price per pound of coffee beans is $1.50, and the six-month futures price is $1.61. Based on a risk-free rate of 1%, we can infer the net cost-of-carry from the cost-of-carry relationship: $F_0 = S_0 \times (1 + r_f + c)^T => c = 14.2\%$. If we use $ln(1 + 1\%)$ as the risk-free rate and $-ln(1 + 14.2\%)$ as the dividend yield in the Black-Scholes model (because the model requires *continuous* rates) along with a volatility for coffee bean returns of 25%, we can use an online options calculator to find the premia (i.e., values) for call and put options with exercise prices of $1.50 and six months to maturity of $0.173 and $0.063, respectively. Check it for yourself.

8.3 Long vs. short option positions

If we **buy** a call or a put option, we take **long** positions, and if we **sell** (which in the option terminology is called "write") a call or put option, we take **short** positions. However, in the case of put options, this is a bit deceptive. For example, a long put option is a right to sell, and unlike long positions in general, a long put option decreases in value with the underlying asset price. Thus, we will see later that a *long* asset position can be effectively hedged with a *long put*. More discussion is warranted to clear up this confusion.

First, however, let me introduce the graphs of intrinsic values in Figure 8.3. For the two long positions on top, the solid lines give the intrinsic values, whereas the dashed lines give the intrinsic values less the option premium that we paid

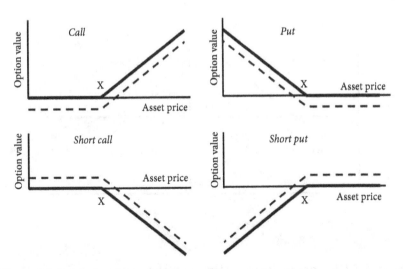

Figure 8.3 Intrinsic values of option positions

for the option. The two short positions on the bottom show mirror images of the long positions, because these positions are zero-sum games in that whatever the buyers of the options gain, the sellers lose, and vice versa.

8.4 Alternative option strategies to hedge a <u>long</u> asset position

This section discusses several ways to use options as a hedge for a long asset position, such as owning a stock. Figure 8.4 depicts a long position.

To hedge this long position with a positive slope, we need to identify an offsetting option position with a negative slope. Among the four available option positions, either buying a put or writing a call fits the bill. These two positions are shaded in Figure 8.5.

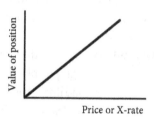

Figure 8.4 Long position

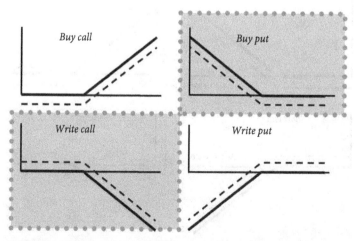

Figure 8.5 Offsetting positions to a long position

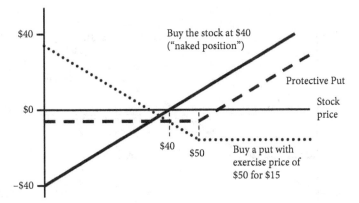

Figure 8.6 Protective put

Let us first examine the most traditional hedge, which is to buy a put option to hedge a long position. We start with a stock that costs us $40 (the actual purchasing price of this stock is inconsequential here). To hedge the stock position, we buy a put on the same stock with an exercise price of $50 for $15. The solid line in Figure 8.6 shows the value of the stock position (net of the $40 cost), while the dotted line shows the intrinsic value of the put position (net of the $15 cost). Combining the two positions gives a portfolio consisting of one stock and one put option on the stock and is called a *protective put* position. The dashed line in the graph shows that this position has a limited downside; in the worst-case scenario, we lose only $5.[3] In this case, we see that the put option does not eliminate risk—we still retain a lot of upside potential—but it protects against the downside. In that sense, it is much like buying old-fashioned insurance.

We could alternatively buy a put option with an exercise price of $20 for $2, as shown in Figure 8.7. While this put option is much cheaper, it also offers less protection, in that the worst-case scenario gives a loss of $22. This is like buying cheaper insurance with a larger deductible.

Selling a call option would be a less traditional hedge in this case. Nevertheless, suppose that we sell a call option with an exercise price of $50

[3] Oh, don't be confused that the protective put position looks like a plain call option. Incidentally, this is what gives rise to the so-called *put-call parity* that formalizes the relation between the values of call options and put options. But enough about that here.

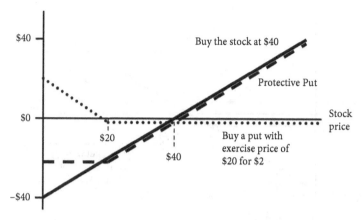

Figure 8.7 Cheap protective put

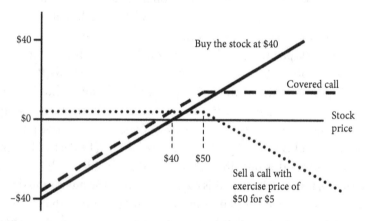

Figure 8.8 Covered call

for $5. The combination of the long stock and the short call gives a *covered call* position. Figure 8.8 shows that the covered call position "sweetens the downside" compared to the unhedged position, because we get to keep the option premium on the unexercised option when the stock price drops. You can think of this as a consolation prize. However, the protection is rather modest, making it less appealing as a hedging tool. Many managers also dislike that it chops off the upside potential, as the buyer of the options exercises when the stock price increases.

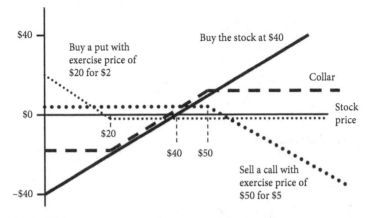

Figure 8.9 Collar

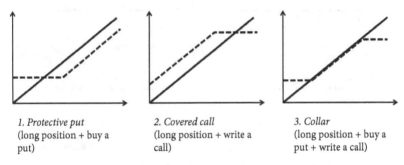

1. Protective put
(long position + buy a
put)

2. Covered call
(long position + write a
call)

3. Collar
(long position + buy a
put + write a call)

Figure 8.10 Alternative hedges for a long position

A third hedge is to combine the strategies of buying a put *and* selling a call to get a *collar* position. In the typical collar, the exercise price of the call is higher than the put, and sometimes the premiums are chosen to be similar so that the sale of the call essentially pays for the purchase of the put and we get a *costless collar*. In Figure 8.9, we buy a put with an exercise price of $20 for $2 and sell a call with an exercise price of $50 for $5. As a result, the put option protects the downside while the collar chops off the upside, and in between the premiums offset each other. Incidentally, if we buy a put option and sell a call option with the same exercise prices, we remove all risk, just like a futures contract. I have not drawn such a special collar here, but you can try it on your own.

In summary, we can hedge a long position with a protective put, covered call, or a collar, as shown in Figure 8.10

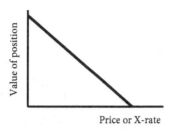

Figure 8.11 Short position

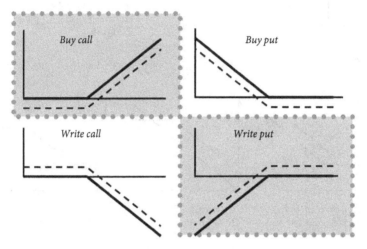

Figure 8.12 Offsetting positions to a short position

8.5 Alternative option strategies to hedge a <u>short</u> asset position

Using options to hedge a short asset position is essentially the opposite of using options to hedge a long asset position. Figure 8.11 depicts a short position.

To hedge this short asset position with a negative slope, we need to identify an offsetting option position with a positive slope. Among the four available option positions, either buying a call or writing a put should work and are shaded in Figure 8.12.

Using a long call to hedge the short position yields a *protective call*, which protects against large price increases. Using a short put to hedge the short position yields a *covered put*, which sweetens the downside when prices

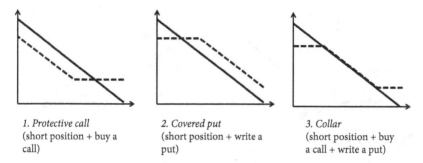

1. *Protective call*
(short position + buy a
call)

2. *Covered put*
(short position + write a
put)

3. *Collar*
(short position + buy
a call + write a put)

Figure 8.13 Alternative hedges for a short position

increase. Last, using both a long call and a short put to hedge the short position, where the exercise price of the call exceeds that of the put, yields a *collar*,
which protects against large price increases but also removes some upside
potential. Figure 8.13 depicts these hedging strategies.

8.6 Delta hedging

The delta of an option is the change in its value for a unit (i.e., $1) change in
the underlying asset. Thus, it is the slope of the total option value graph at
the current price. The first graph in Figure 8.14 describes this for a call option that is currently at-the-money (that is, the current price S_0 exceeds the
exercise price X). If the price were to increase, the slope increases, and vice
versa. The delta for a <u>call</u> option is between 0 and 1. In contrast, the delta
for a <u>put</u> option is between −1 and 0, as is evident from the second graph in
Figure 8.14.

Suppose now that you hold 100 shares of SPY (an ETF on the S&P 500) on
June 9, 2015, with a value of 100 × $208.70 = $20,870. You are concerned
about a value drop over the summer and would like to enter an options
hedge. Let us focus on a put option with X = $200 that expires on September
18. With a short-term risk-free rate of 0.02%, volatility of 16%, and dividend
yield of 1.9%, the option should be selling for about $4.13. (You can search for
a Black-Scholes option calculator online to verify this put option premium.)
Also, the put option delta is −0.324. (Again, you can verify this for yourself
using an online option calculator.) The put option delta gives the slope of the
graph for the put option premium at the current SPY price, and, therefore,
indicates how much the put option premium changes for a $1 change in the

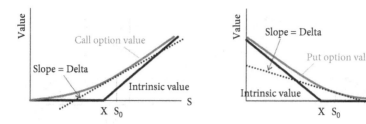

Figure 8.14 Option deltas

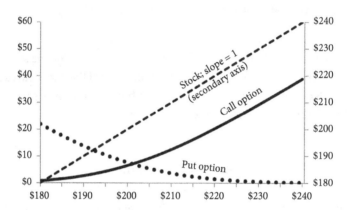

Figure 8.15 Call and put options on SPY

SPY price. Put option premiums, as well as premiums for a call option with the same exercise price and maturity, are depicted below for SPY prices between $180 and $240. Figure 8.15 shows these options.

Suppose that the SPY price drops by $1 to $207.70, such that the 100 shares of SPY drop in value by $100. Then the put option premium should increase by approximately –$1 × –0.324 = $0.324 to a premium of $4.45. If you bought options to cover the 100 shares of SPY, the option portfolio would increase in value by $32.40.

Interestingly, while the put option hedge is really designed to provide protection when the price falls below $200 (the exercise price), the value of the option increases even as the price drops from only $208.70 to $207.70. Thus, the put option can be used to provide value protection for a larger range than just the tail. But, as the numbers indicate, to provide full value protection, you would have to acquire roughly 300 options, such that their value increase would be $32.40 × 3 = $97.20.

This brings us to *delta hedging*, where the objective is to acquire enough options to provide full value protection, even if the price of the stock does

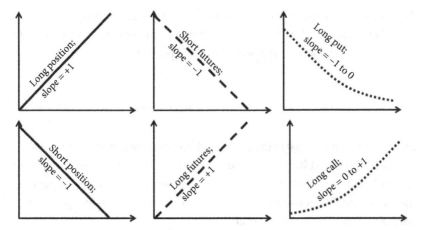

Figure 8.16 The use of futures vs. options to hedge

not dip below the exercise price. This is similar to the objective when using a futures/forward contract—which is to <u>eliminate</u> all risk—but different from the objective when most companies use options—which is to <u>insure against the downside risk</u> (i.e., eliminate just the risk in the downside tail).

Figure 8.16 illustrates the use of futures/forwards vs. options to hedge against changes in the value of either a long or short position. Using futures contracts to hedge changes in the value of our original position, we can remove all risk. And because the slopes are equally steep, the underlying quantity in the original position and the futures contract should be the same. We can alternatively use options to hedge changes in the value. But we need to increase the quantity underlying the option contracts to account for the gentler slope (similar to what we did earlier with cross hedging).

How much should we increase the number of underlying options to account for the gentler slope? That is, what is the optimal *hedge ratio*?

If we start with an <u>option portfolio</u> and would like to hedge the risk using the underlying stock (or other asset), the optimal *hedge ratio* equals *delta*. But that is not very relevant, because it is rare for us to start with an option portfolio that we would like to hedge. If we instead start with a <u>stock portfolio</u> and would like to hedge the risk using options on the stock, the optimal *hedge ratio* equals *1/delta*. Thus, the optimal hedge ratio in the earlier SPY example was 1/0.324 = 3.09, and we should buy 3.09 × 100 = 309 options to hedge our position.

However, as the price of the underlying asset changes, so does the delta. In our example, the drop in the SPY price of $1 would cause the delta of our put option to change to –0.344, and the new optimal hedge ratio falls to 2.91.

Thus, to retain the delta hedge, we should sell 309 − 291 = 18 options. As you probably understand by now, delta hedging requires continuous "rebalancing" (buying and selling of options) to work perfectly.

8.7 Options vs. insurance

Insurance can be viewed as derivatives where the underlying asset is the value of any loss suffered by the insured party. In particular, buying put options when already owning the underlying asset is similar to buying insurance on the asset, and protective puts are sometimes referred to as portfolio insurance. But there are important differences:

- Asset specificity: Derivatives are tied to market prices of commodities, and anyone exposed to those market prices can use derivatives as a hedging tool. In contrast, insurance is tied to the loss of a very particular asset (e.g., a specific house), and only the owner of that asset can use insurance to hedge against a potential loss of that asset. As a result, insurance is plagued with adverse selection and moral hazard.
- Hedge accuracy: Derivatives rarely provide a perfect hedge because changes in the commodity value rarely match changes in the hedger's position perfectly due to basis risk. Insurance provides a close hedge against losses on a certain asset, especially when contractual uncertainties, deductibles, and co-insurance are low.
- Contracting costs: Whereas the contracting costs for derivatives are typically small, they can be substantial for insurance. That is, insurance companies incur large costs from information gathering and analysis, monitoring, adverse selection, and moral hazard, and they will pass these costs on to the customers in the form of higher insurance premiums.
- Liquidity: The liquidity is much higher for derivatives, and the higher liquidity is useful if there is a potential need to unwind a hedge.

8.8 Options vs. futures and forwards

If we hedge a position using forwards or futures where (i) the horizon of the hedge matches the expiration of the contracts and (ii) the underlying assets of the unhedged position and the contracts are identical, the risk is eliminated. But even if the same two conditions hold when we use options to hedge the position, the risk is generally not eliminated. Rather, option hedges merely protect against or sweeten the most adverse scenarios. Exceptions include collars in which (a) the exercise prices of the call and put options are identical, which is essentially the same as forwards/futures, and (b) delta hedging with options.

If forwards and futures remove more risk than options, are options an inferior hedging tool? Not necessarily. The goal of hedging should <u>not</u> be to reduce as much risk as possible. Rather, the primary goal of hedging should be to dodge the ripple effects that accompany cash shortfalls and allow the firm to pursue positive NPV projects. It is conceivable that option hedges do this more effectively.

Another explanation for the popularity of option hedges is that they are motivated by managers' preferences to preserve the upside potential, especially when they believe that commodity prices will move in their favor. In that sense, it is related to the earlier discussion on selective hedging and overconfidence.

A related explanation is that managers fear that they might end up looking foolish if they use futures/forwards. If they hedge using either futures/forwards or options and the prices move against them, they end up looking smart. In contrast, if the prices move in their favor, they end up looking foolish if they hedged using futures/forwards (even though the company is still fine), but smart if they hedged using options, because the firm retained the upside in the latter case. Unfortunately, this logic means that managers might use options to hedge against themselves looking foolish instead of choosing the mechanism that might be most suitable for the company.

8.9 An analogy: The fear of looking foolish in football

Making suboptimal decisions to avoid looking foolish might be more widespread than we would like to think. Consider penalty kicks in football (yes, I insist on calling it football instead of soccer again), as illustrated in Figure 8.17. Professional goalkeepers remain in the center of the goal only a small fraction of the time, probably less than 5%. Why? Perhaps to show that they are at least making an effort, and standing still when the ball goes to one side looks rather ridiculous, right? In any event, this means that it

Figure 8.17 Penalty kick in football

makes sense for the striker to shoot in the center of the goal. In fact, the empirical evidence suggests that the success rate of penalty shots is higher for those that target the higher part of the goal, and penalty shots that target the high center of the goal enjoy the highest success rate. (To see some elegant examples, search for "Panenka" at youtube.com.) Why don't strikers use this statistic to their advantage and shoot more often high in the middle? Likely because the minority of those shots that are saved by goalkeepers who stand still make the strikers look very foolish. And, unlike an unsuccessful shot in the low corner, the striker is blamed for a pitiful effort.

9

Hedging-Simulations

9.1 The use of simulations as a hedging tool

Simulations are effective for assessing the effect of hedging alternatives. In this section, we will simulate cash flow or cash levels under different hedging alternatives and primarily examine how the *left tail* of the distributions differs. For example, what is the probability of a cash shortfall under different alternatives?

Given the general focus on expected values when undertaking valuations, there is a natural temptation to focus on the *average* cash level in the simulations. However, we will not actually include the costs associated with ripple effects in the simulations—we just know that these costs arise for low cash levels, and we therefore seek to minimize the probability of such low cash levels. Consequently, any differences in the average cash level across the hedging alternatives are due to one of the following possibilities:

- The hedging instruments are unfairly priced. Sometimes tailor-made hedging instruments are quite expensive—after all, financial institutions providing such tailor-made instruments are in business to make money. And even exchange-traded products can be "mispriced" if there is an imbalance of supply and demand, for example, as a result of more hedgers on either the long or short side (refer to the earlier discussion of contango and backwardation).
- Hedging alters the company's systematic risk. If the underlying assets have systematic risk, derivatives on the assets also have systematic risk (this is also related to the earlier discussion of contango and backwardation). When a firm acquires such derivatives, it will acquire the systematic risk. This, in turn, affects the firm's cost of capital. Thus, an increase in the average cash level likely comes with an increase in systematic risk and vice versa, and the two changes have offsetting effects on the value.
- The simulation is based on inconsistent assumptions or contains some other mistake.

Applied Corporate Risk and Liquidity Management. Erik Lie, Oxford University Press. © Oxford University Press 2023.
DOI: 10.1093/oso/9780197664995.003.0009

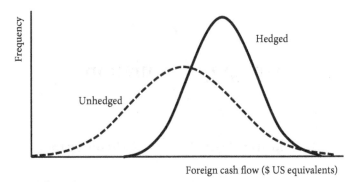

Figure 9.1 Example of hedged positions for Merck

Thus, I mainly examine the differences in the average cash levels for indications that there is some error in the simulations. Large differences are almost certainly attributable to some error that I must correct. But much lower average values for alternatives that use hedging could also arise if we pay unfairly steep prices for hedging instruments. (We should be able to detect this with some fairly basic derivatives valuation skills.) Small differences can be attributable to modest mispricing or changes in systematic risk, and I do not worry about them. Regardless, *you should be wary of basing hedging decisions on differences in average simulated cash levels!*

A useful lesson can be learned from an article by Lewent and Kearney (1990) that describes how Merck used simulations to examine the effect of hedging. The article contains a graph very similar to the one in Figure 9.1 and the discussion below.

> The quarterly cash flow information for each of a large number of scenarios is collected and displayed graphically in frequency plots, and in terms of statistics such as means, standard deviations, and confidence levels. Exhibit 9 [the graph] provides an example of the graphical output from our simulator, comparing distributions of unhedged and hedged cash flows. In this case, the hedged curve assumes 100% of Merck's exposure has been covered through the purchase of foreign currency options. Given the pattern of exchange rate movements simulated, the hedging strategy has shifted the hedged cash flow distribution to the right, cutting off a portion of unfavorable outcomes. In addition, the hedged cash flow distribution has a higher mean value as well as a lower standard deviation. Therefore, in this scenario

hedging would be preferable to not hedging, resulting in higher returns as well as lower risk. (Again, of course, the trade-off is the initial cost of the option premiums that would have to be balanced against the improved risk/return pattern.)

Based on the article, Merck's hedging entails the purchase of options. The article further points out that hedging triggers a substantial increase in the average foreign cash flow, and for this reason (along with the lower standard deviation), "hedging would be preferable to not hedging."

There is no indication that Merck's simulation reflects any ripple effects. What is causing the increase in the average cash flow then? The last sentence of the article excerpt gives a clue: "Again, of course, the trade-off is the initial cost of the option premiums that would have to be balanced against the improved risk/return pattern." In other words, the analysis ignores the cost of the options. Or put differently, the option premiums were set to zero. This is a gross mispricing. Any investor who gets free options is naturally better off, but this is unreasonable and deceptive because options are rarely free. Thus, Merck's hedging recommendation is based on flawed premises.

Another curiosity about the graph is that, while hedging makes the distribution noticeably narrower, the symmetry is preserved. We will see in later examples that hedging strategies based on purchasing options make the distribution asymmetric. Thus, I am at a loss for what is going on in the Merck analysis, except that there appear to be several serious flaws, rendering the analysis useless.

9.2 A simple exchange rate example

A US company is scheduled to receive €500,000 in six months, and it is considering hedging against exchange rate fluctuations. The current exchange rate is \$1.126/€, and the six-month futures price is \$1.128/€. Option premiums (per € in the contract) are as follows:

	X = \$1.070	X = \$1.120	X = \$1.170
Call option	\$0.067	\$0.035	\$0.015
Put option	\$0.011	\$0.029	\$0.059

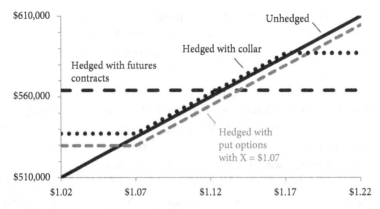

Figure 9.2 Hedging exchange rate exposure

Incidentally, buying a put option and selling a call option with an exercise price of $1.12 effectively locks in a price of $1.12 − $0.029 + $0.035 = $1.126.[1] This should have been very similar to the futures price, but in this case, it is a bit lower, and, thus, the put/call combination is an inferior alternative to the plain futures contract. You can think of this as some slight mispricing.

Figure 9.2 shows how much the company would receive in US dollars for different exchange rates in six months if it (1) remains unhedged, (2) hedges with futures contracts, (3) hedges with put options with X = $1.07, and (4) hedges with a collar that has put options with X = $1.07 and call options with X = $1.17. This is a common way for textbooks to display the outcomes. While this is informative, it ignores the distribution of the future exchange rates. I assumed that there is no expected drift in the exchange rate during the next six months, but that the monthly standard deviation in the exchange rate returns is 3%. This means that the six-month standard deviation is roughly 3% × √6 = 7.3% and the yearly standard deviation is roughly 3% × √12 = 10.4%, and we get the distribution of exchange rates after six months given in Figure 9.3.

If I use the exchange rate distribution as an assumption in Crystal Ball, and then simulate the US dollar values received under the unhedged and three hedged alternatives, I get the distributions in Figure 9.4. Note that because of the discontinuities in the hedged distributions, I chose to represent those with columns instead of lines.

---

[1] Other combinations using call and put options with the same exercise price give the same effective price of $1.126.

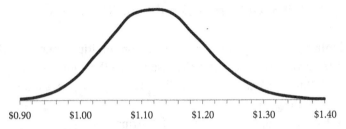

Figure 9.3 Exchange rate distribution

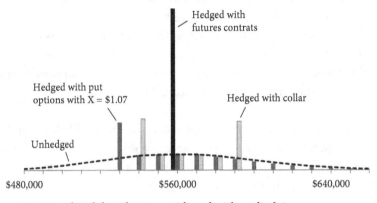

Figure 9.4 Simulated distributions with and without hedging

The distributions show the following:

- The bulk of the unhedged values fall between $480,000 and $660,000. (Closer inspection of the underlying trial values reveals that 99% fall between $466,000 and $673,000.)
- Hedging with futures contracts locks in the value at roughly $560,000 ($564,000 to be precise).
- Hedging with put options removes the left tail, such that the lowest value is at roughly $530,000, where we see a large chunk of the distribution.
- Hedging with the collar also removes the left tail, such that the lowest value is at roughly $540,000. (The higher lowest value compared to the one for using the protective put is due to the income from selling the call options for $0.015 × 500,000 = $7,500.) In addition, the collar removes the right tail, such that the highest value is roughly $590,000.
- The average values are roughly the same, which is comforting, because large discrepancies would have been indicative of errors. This might not be evident from the graph, but it is verified by calculating averages of the underlying trial values.

9.3 Gold mine simulation: The basics

A gold mining company faces uncertainty from multiple sources, including gold prices, production, etc. I initially assume that these uncertainties are uncorrelated. But in an extension, we will explore what happens if investments increase with the gold price.

Some basic assumptions include the following:

- The gold price is currently $1,200, and it is expected to increase 1% per year, with a standard deviation of 15%.
- Production is expected to increase 12% next year and 5% in the year thereafter, with standard deviations of 5% and 3%, respectively.
- Several balance sheet items are a fraction of COGS rather than revenues, such that they are not affected by the gold price.

Historical and projected financial statements are provided below. All dollar values except the price and cost per ounce of gold are in millions. As earlier, we will focus on cash balances in future years to ensure sufficient liquidity and, thereby, dodge ripple effects.

	2020	2021	2022E	2023E
Market price of gold	$1,150	$1,200	$1,212	$1,224
Production—ounces of gold	5,064,000	5,154,000	5,772,480	6,061,104
Cost per oz.	$714	$744	$759	$774
Revenues	$5,824	$6,185	$6,996	$7,420
COGS	$3,616	$3,835	$4,381	$4,692
Other expenses	$1,777	$1,804	$1,840	$1,877
	$431	$546	$776	$851
Taxes (30%)	$129	$164	$233	$255
Net income	$302	$382	$543	$596
Dividend	$100	$110	$116	$121
Retained earnings	$202	$272	$427	$474

	2020	2021	2022E	2023E
Cash and cash equivalents	$1,153	$1,425	$735	$739
Accounts receivable	$231	$240	$307	$328
Inventory	$1,235	$1,130	$1,533	$1,642
Other current assets	$667	$711	$964	$1,032
Current assets	$3,286	$3,506	$3,538	$3,742
PP&E	$8,613	$9,433	$9,905	$10,202
Goodwill	$5,241	$5,429	$5,538	$5,648
Other assets	$1,810	$1,846	$1,883	$1,921
Total assets	$18,950	$20,214	$20,864	$21,512
Accounts payable	$512	$764	$876	$938
Short-term debt	$231	$240	$245	$250
Other current liabilities	$255	$270	$275	$281
Current liabilities	$998	$1,274	$1,396	$1,469
Long-term debt	$2,665	$3,356	$3,423	$3,492
Other liabilities	$1,598	$1,623	$1,655	$1,689
Total liabilities	$5,261	$6,253	$6,475	$6,649
Capital stock	$11,835	$11,835	$11,835	$11,835
Retained earnings	$1,854	$2,126	$2,554	$3,028
Total equity	$13,689	$13,961	$14,389	$14,863
Total liabilities and equity	$18,950	$20,214	$20,864	$21,512

To run simulations, I created columns for the simulated numbers, and columns for the means and standard deviations for the normal distributions used in the simulations. For example, the spreadsheet snapshot below indicates that the growth in gold price for 2022 is distributed normally with a mean of 1% and a standard deviation of 15%. As always, Crystal Ball has colored all the cells with assumptions green and the output variables (i.e., the cash balances) turquoise.

Incidentally, I have included some uncertainty in the short-term and long-term debt figures as well. However, one could argue that these figures are largely dictated by contracts or our decisions, and, as such, should be largely certain.

	2022E	2023E		Simulation '22E	Simulation '23E	Mean '22E	Mean '23E	Std. dev. '22E	Std. dev. '23E
Market price of gold	$1,212	$1,224	Growth	1%	1%	1%	1%	15%	15%
Forward prices of gold	$1,212	$1,224	Forw. prem. (annual)			1%	1%		
Forw. price next yr. (sim.)		$1,224	Forw. prem. next year		1%		1%		1%
Put prem. (X = $1100)	$29	$50							
Call prem. (X = $1300)	$36	$69							
Production (oz of gold)	5,772,480	6,061,104	Growth	12%	5%	12%	5%	5%	3%
Cost per oz.	$759	$774	Growth	2%	2%	2%	2%	4%	2%
Revenues	$6,996	$7,420							
COGS	$4,381	$4,692							
Other expenses	$1,840	$1,877	Growth	2%	2%	2%	2%	2%	2%
Cost of derivatives	$0	$0							
Hedging gain	$0	$0							
	$776	$851							
Taxes (30%)	$233	$255							
Net income	$543	$596							
Dividend	$116	$121	Growth			5%	5%		
Retained earnings	$427	$474							

			PLUG						
Cash and equivalents	$735	$739							
Accounts receivable	$307	$328	Fr. of COGS	7%	7%	7%	7%	1%	1%
Inventory	$1,533	$1,642	Fr. of COGS	35%	35%	35%	35%	3%	3%
Other current assets	$964	$1,032	Fr. of COGS	22%	22%	22%	22%	1%	1%
Current assets	$3,538	$3,742							
PP&E	$9,905	$10,202	Growth	5%	3%	3%	3%	1%	1%
Goodwill	$5,538	$5,648	Growth	2%	2%	2%	2%	1%	1%
Other assets	$1,883	$1,921	Growth	2%	2%	2%	2%	1%	1%
Total assets	$20,864	$21,512							
Accounts payable	$876	$938	Fr. of COGS	20%	20%	20%	20%	2%	2%
Short-term debt	$245	$250	Growth	2%	2%	2%	2%	1%	1%
Other current liabil.	$275	$281	Growth	2%	2%	2%	2%	1%	1%
Current liabilities	$1,396	$1,469							
Long-term debt	$3,423	$3,492	Growth	2%	2%	2%	2%	1%	1%
Other liabilities	$1,655	$1,689	Growth	2%	2%	2%	2%	1%	1%
Total liabilities	$6,475	$6,649							
Capital stock	$11,835	$11,835							
Retained earnings	$2,554	$3,028							
Total equity	$14,389	$14,863							
Total liabil. and equity	$20,864	$21,512							

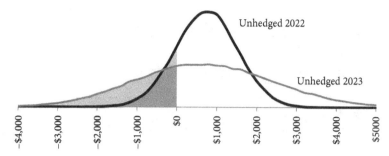

Figure 9.5 Unhedged cash distributions

The initial simulations assume that the company does not engage in any hedging activities. Figure 9.5 shows the simulated cash distributions in the next two years. The means of the distributions are both positive, indicating that the company is expected to have positive cash balances in both years. However, both distributions, and especially the one for 2023, stretch well into negative territory. In fact, the probability of a cash shortfall in 2022 is 17%, and it doubles to 34% in 2023. On this basis, it appears that the company is in great danger of incurring ripple effects from cash shortages.

9.4 Gold mine simulation: Enter derivatives

The next stage examines how hedging affects the cash distributions. The hedging instruments include forward contracts, put options with an exercise price of $1,100, and call options with an exercise price of $1,300. I examine the following hedging strategies:

- Forward contracts
  - A one-year forward contract is entered today to sell the expected production in 2022.
  - A two-year forward contract is entered today to sell the expected production in 2023.
  - I also made an adjustment for the 2023 hedge based on the production in 2022. In particular, if the production in 2022 is higher (lower) than expected, the expected production for 2023 will also be higher (lower), and the forward contracts for 2023 are increased (decreased) correspondingly.[2]

---

[2] This has a trivial effect, and you may ignore this if it gives you a headache. I primarily made the adjustment to facilitate comparison with the rolling forward contracts that I discuss later.

- Put options
  - o A one-year put option with an exercise price of $1,100 is bought today to cover the expected production in 2022.
  - o A two-year put option with an exercise price of $1,100 is bought today to cover the expected production in 2023.
- Collar
  - o A one-year put option with an exercise price of $1,100 is bought *and* a one-year call option with an exercise price of $1,300 is sold today to cover the expected production in 2022.
  - o A two-year put option with an exercise price of $1,100 is bought *and* a two-year call option with an exercise price of $1,300 is sold today to cover the expected production in 2023.

To implement the hedging strategies, I created three sets of rows in the spreadsheet:

(1) A set of rows where I can enter the fraction of production hedged using the different derivatives. This allows me to readily see which hedging alternative I have assumed (e.g., a 100% forward hedge) and facilitates changing my hedging alternative by simply altering the fractions in these rows.

(2) A set of rows that calculates the hedged production, that is, the product of the *expected* production and the fraction of production hedged. Students often get confused about why I use the expected production here, and not the actual production. The reason is that we enter the derivatives contracts at a time when the actual production is not known yet. So it is entirely possible that we intend to hedge 100% of our production against price changes, but because our production is, say, 11% higher than expected, we end up hedging only 90% (100/111) of the actual production.

(3) A set of rows that calculates the premium paid/received for options and the gains from derivatives upon expiration. Incidentally, while the premium is calculated under the column for the year of the option expirations, it is assumed to be paid/received in the beginning of 2022.

The snapshot below shows the calculations if I select to hedge 50% of the production in each of the next two years with long-term forward contracts and the remaining 50% of the production with put options. Incidentally,

I do not examine this combo hedging strategy—it is only shown for illustration purposes. To only hedge using, say, forward contracts, I could simply change the percentages on the forward contracts row to 100% and set the others to 0%.

	2022E	2023E	
Fraction of expected production hedged			
Forward contracts	50%	50%	
Put options (X = $1100)	50%	50%	
Write call options (X = $1300)	0%	0%	
Expected production	5,772,480	6,061,104	
Hedged production			
Forward contracts	2,886,240	3,030,552	H_1
Put options	2,886,240	3,030,552	H_2
Write call options	0	0	H_3
Tot. prem. paid (received) for options	$84	$152	→ "Cost of derivatives" in income statement (IS)
Gains			
LT forward contracts	$0	$0	$(F-P)*H_1$
Put options	$0	$0	$MAX(0,X-P)*H_2$
Write call options	$0	$0	$-MAX(0,X-P)*H_3$
Total	$0	$0	→ "Hedging gain" in IS

The total premium paid (received) for options is calculated as the difference between the premium paid for put options that we buy and the premium received for the call options that we sell: [H_2 (oz of gold in the put option contracts) × put option premium] − [H_3 (oz of gold in the call contracts) × call option premium]. The illustration above only includes the purchase of put options, so for 2022 the total premium paid is simply 2,886,240 × $29 = $84 million.

The formula for estimating the value of the gains for the LT forward contracts in the spreadsheet is:

$$=(F-P)*H_1$$

where P refers to the simulated gold price, F is the forward price ($1,212 for forwards that expire in 2022 and $1,224 for forwards that expire in 2023), and H_1 is the hedged production using long-term forward contracts. In the snapshot above, P = F, so the value of the gain is given as $0. If the simulated P were to drop to $1,000 in 2022, the gain would be given as ($1,212 – $1,000) × 2,886,240 = $612 million.

The formula for estimating the value of the gains for the put options in the spreadsheet is:

$$=MAX(0,X-P)*H_2$$

where P is the simulated gold price, X is the exercise price of the put options ($1,100), and H_2 is the hedged production using put options. In the snapshot above, P>X, so the value of the gain is given as $0. If the simulated P were to drop to $1,000 in 2022, the gain would be given as ($1,100 – $1,000) × 2,886,240 = $289 million.

The formula for estimating the value of the gains for the short call options (i.e., write call options) in the spreadsheet is:

$$=-MAX(0,P-X)*H_3$$

where P is the simulated gold price, X is the exercise price of the call options ($1,300), and H_3 is the hedged production using call options. Note that $=-MAX(\cdot)$ is not the same as $=MIN(\cdot)$, a common misconception among students.

Of course, we then must transfer the premium paid for the put options to the income statement where it shows up as "Cost of derivatives." We also transfer the gains upon expiration, which obviously depend on the simulated gold price, to the income statement where they show up as "Hedging gain." And then we can run our simulation with hedging.

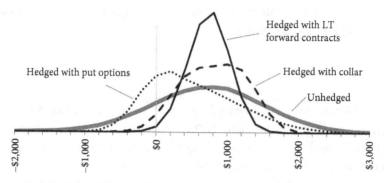

Figure 9.6 Cash distributions for 2022

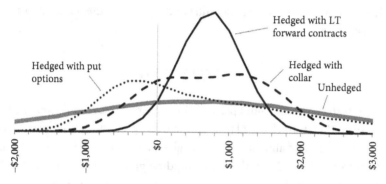

Figure 9.7 Cash distributions for 2023

Now, let us look at the simulation results. Figure 9.6 shows the cash distributions for the various hedging strategies for 2022, while Figure 9.7 shows the distributions for 2023. The primary takeaway is that the hedging strategies generally reduce the probability of a cash shortfall substantially while preserving the average cash balance. We also see that forward contracts tend to remove more risk than options do.

There are also some other results worth noting about the use of options:

- The put option strategy fails to reduce the probability of a cash shortfall. Nevertheless, it reduces the probability of the most negative scenarios (i.e., it chops off the leftmost tail).
- Perhaps more disconcertingly, the average cash balance is lower in 2022 for the put option strategy than for the other strategies. This occurs because the firm must pay the option premiums upfront. That is, the firm

has bought put options to cover the 2023 production, and this premium has depleted the 2022 cash balance. If we were to count the one-year options as a "cash equivalent" (like many liquid instruments are), the average cash balance would be similar for the put option strategy as for the other strategies.

- The average cash balance for the collar strategy is a little higher than for the other strategies in 2022, because the call option premium that the firm receives exceeds the put option premium that it pays. In this case, it is as if the firm has debt in the form of the short call options that is not reflected in the higher cash balance.

9.5 Gold mine simulation: Enter rolling forward contracts

The previous section examined the effect of forward contracts, in particular, the use of a combination of one-year and two-year forward contracts. But long-term contracts, such as two-year contracts, might be unavailable. Thus, in this section I examine the effect of rolling one-year forward contracts instead.

I consider two different rolling forward strategies:

- Rolling forward 1
  - o A one-year forward contract is entered today to sell the expected production in 2022.
  - o A one-year forward contract is entered next year to sell the expected production in 2023.
- Rolling forward 2
  - o A one-year forward contract is entered today to sell the expected production in 2022.
  - o Another one-year forward contract is entered today to sell the expected production in 2023. (The expected production in 2023 is as of the time when the one-year forward contract is entered.)
  - o A one-year forward contract is entered next year to sell the expected production in 2023.

These strategies are depicted in Figure 9.8 along with the strategy from the prior subsection based on long-term (i.e., both one-year and two-year)

Figure 9.8 Rolling forwards for gold mine

forward contracts. As is apparent from the illustration, the first rolling forward contract strategy leaves the gold expected to be produced and sold in 2023 exposed to price variations during 2022 (until we enter forward contracts for this gold). The illustration further shows that the second rolling forward strategy introduces some rollover risk. The simulation results show the consequences of these differences.

Figure 9.9 and Figure 9.10 show the cash distributions from the simulations using the two rolling forward strategies for 2022 and 2023, respectively. For comparison, the graphs also show the cash distribution for the strategy based on the long-term contracts (one-year and two-year contracts) in the previous subsection.

Based on the cash distributions for 2023, we see that the second rolling forward strategy (Rolling forward 2) performs about equally well as the strategy based on longer-term forward contracts. In fact, the two distributions appear to be perfectly overlapping. That suggests that the additional rollover risk embedded in the second rolling forward strategy is negligible. In contrast, the cash distribution using the first rolling forward strategy is wider, suggesting that this strategy is less effective in reducing risk. That should not be surprising, given that it leaves the second-year gold production exposed to price risk during the entire first year.

The cash distributions for 2022 are more curious. For that year, the first rolling forward strategy gives a tighter distribution than the second rolling forward strategy, the opposite of what we say about the cash distributions for 2023. What is going on?

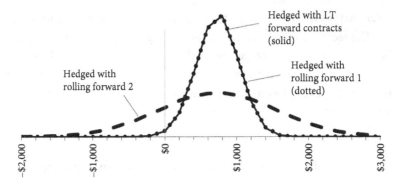

Figure 9.9 Cash distributions with rolling forwards for 2022

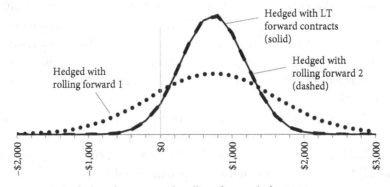

Figure 9.10 Cash distributions with rolling forwards for 2023

It turns out that the distributions for 2022 are a bit misleading. See if you can follow this. What is happening is that, if the gold price increases in 2022, the one-year forward contracts exhibit losses. For the one-year contract covering production in 2022, this loss is offset by the gain in revenues. But for the one-year contract covering production in 2023, there is not yet any off-setting gain in revenues in 2022. Rather, the firm is able to lock in a much higher price with the next one-year forward contract, such that the offsetting gain will effectively occur in 2023. In other words, while there is a loss and a correspondingly lower cash balance in 2022, the firm is perfectly positioned for a higher revenue in 2023. In that sense, the low cash balance is deceptive. (Incidentally, this is really not different from the long-term forward contracts, except that the loss for the long-term contracts as of 2022 is only on paper and not realized. And had the long-term contracts instead been *futures* contracts, the losses would show up in the cash balance for 2022, because the profits and losses are settled daily for such contracts.)

After that convoluted explanation, let me wrap up with a simple summary: The second rolling forward strategy using one-year contracts appears to be almost as effective as the forward strategy using one- and two-year contracts. Conversely, the first rolling forward strategy is noticeably less effective than the other forward strategies, but even this strategy reduces substantial risk.

9.6 Gold mine simulation: An investment wrinkle

It is time to add yet another wrinkle. Suppose that the firm's investment depends on the gold price. That is, suppose that the investment in 2023 depends on the gold price change in 2022. This makes sense, right? If the gold prices fall, mining becomes less appealing, and vice versa. To implement this, I set the growth in PP&E from 2022 to 2023 equal to half of any positive gold price change from 2021 to 2022. The standard deviation of this growth is still set to be 1%.

I should note that if the investments increase, then the production and revenues should also increase with a lag. For simplicity, I assume that any effect that investment increases in 2023 have on production growth occurs after 2023, and, as such, does not show up in the simulation.

With the new wrinkle, the firm is partially *naturally hedged*. Figure 9.11 shows that the unhedged cash distribution for 2023 narrows as a result. Consequently, the need for additional hedging via derivatives is reduced.

To illustrate that the optimal hedge ratio declines when the investment depends on the gold price, I simulated the cash balance in 2023 using

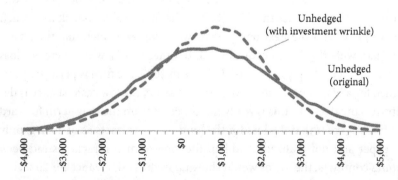

Figure 9.11 Unhedged cash distributions for 2023

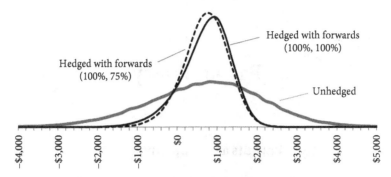

Figure 9.12 Fully and partially hedged cash distributions for 2023

long-term forward contracts covering 100% of the expected production in 2022 and either 100% or 75% of the expected production in 2023. Figure 9.12 displays the simulated cash distributions for 2023. The distribution based on the lower 75% hedge ratio is indeed a bit narrower than the distribution based on the 100% hedge ratio for 2023.

The gold mine simulation serves as a good illustration on how we can identify the optimal hedging strategy amid complex relationships and practical considerations. But, as always, the simulation results are only as helpful as the assumptions are reasonable. Thus, we should spend substantial time and resources in developing our assumptions.

Let me conclude with a concept check for you to deliberate. If the firm instead used put options with an exercise price of $1,000, how would the cash distributions compare to those for the put options with an exercise price of $1,100 used above? (If you want to implement this in the simulation, you can use a one-year option premium of $10 and a two-year premium of $24.)

10

Payout Policy

10.1 Payouts as a supplementary tool

Much of our earlier discussion focused on cash levels. In fact, I have emphasized the use of a cash cushion to avoid ripple effects associated with cash shortages. Furthermore, while it is possible to reduce market and commodity risk using various derivatives, it is difficult to reduce idiosyncratic risk substantially. Thus, we must think of ways to retain a sufficient cash cushion. This is where payout policy becomes an important element.

10.2 Types of payouts

There are two major types of cash disbursements in the form of dividends:

(i) *Regular dividends*—the vast majority of which occur on a quarterly basis
(ii) *Special dividends*—also called extra or year-end dividends

Figure 10.1 presents the aggregate quarterly dividends and special dividends in billions by year paid by US public companies. Clearly, quarterly dividends dominate, representing more than 95% of the total dividends paid. Incidentally, the spike in special dividends in 2004 is due to a tax cut on dividends in 2003.

Figure 10.2 displays the dividends scaled by the market value of the equity at the end of the year. This is essentially the aggregate dividend yield. While total dividends grew in the 1990s, the market value grew more rapidly, such that the dividend yield fell from about 3% to 1% by 2000. Consequently, in the beginning of the current century, leading scholars were talking about the "disappearing dividends." But since the bottom in 2000, the dividend yield has increased and has been hovering around 1.5% to 2%.

Applied Corporate Risk and Liquidity Management. Erik Lie, Oxford University Press. © Oxford University Press 2023.
DOI: 10.1093/oso/9780197664995.003.0010

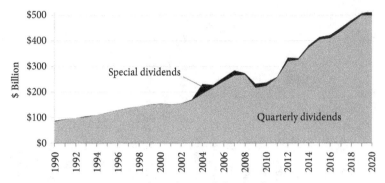

Figure 10.1 Aggregate quarterly and special dividends

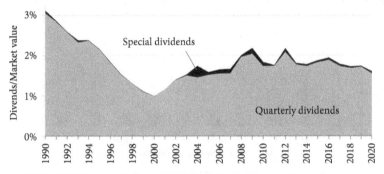

Figure 10.2 Quarterly and special dividends scaled by market value

The main difference between regular and special dividends is that the former creates a long-term commitment. When a special dividend is paid, the implicit understanding is that it is a one-time transaction that will not be repeated anytime soon. But when a quarterly dividend is paid, the understanding is that a similar, or perhaps even larger, dividend will be paid the next quarter.

Figure 10.3 shows the distribution of the year-to-year changes in the quarterly dividend each year (not including dividend initiations and omissions). In 40% of the cases, the quarterly dividends do not change from one year to the next; in 57% of the cases, they increase; and in only 4% of the cases do they decrease. In other words, quarterly dividends tend to either remain constant or increase, illustrating the embedded commitment in such dividends. We will see that this commitment has important implications for the choice of dividends.

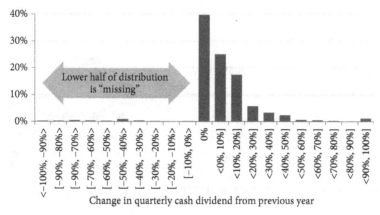

Figure 10.3 Distribution of year-to-year changes in quarterly dividends

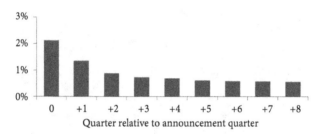

Figure 10.4 Share repurchases scaled by market value after announcements

There are five major types of cash disbursements in the form of share repurchases:

(i) *Open market repurchases (OMRs)*:

OMRs are the most common type of repurchases. Firms periodically announce OMR programs indicating that they might repurchase shares in the open market from time to time during the next couple of years. The plans are rather vague on purpose, thus affording great flexibility. In fact, firms are <u>not committed</u> to complete the repurchases under the OMR plan, and they often end up not repurchasing any shares at all. Figure 10.4, which shows the average share repurchases scaled by market value of equity during the two years after OMR announcements in 1981–2000, illustrates how OMRs are spread over time.

(ii) *Self-tender offers (STOs):*

STOs are relatively rare, but they make a big splash. They are used to repurchase a large chunk of shares, say 10% of the outstanding, within a short time. Firms can announce either a fixed price, or more commonly these days, a range of prices (in which case we refer to the STO as a modified Dutch auction), and invite shareholders to tender their shares (along with the price they request in the case of a Dutch auction) by a given date about one month later.[1] The majority of STOs result in the firms repurchasing the number of shares they requested, but in some cases (primarily if the stock price rises during the tender period) only a few shares are tendered, in which case the offer might be canceled.

(iii) *Rule 10b5-1 preset repurchases:*

Preset repurchases allow firms and insiders to sell a predetermined number of shares at a predetermined time, thus avoiding accusations of insider trading. The downside (at least relative to OMRs) is that flexibility is lost; when firms and insiders adopt preset repo plans, they are committed to repurchase.

(iv) *Accelerated share repurchases (ASRs):*

In ASRs, firms repurchase the shares from an investment bank, which in turn borrows the shares from clients or other investors. This means that the investment bank will have to buy the shares in the open market, perhaps over several months, to return to the lender. A potential advantage for the firm is the faster pace compared to OMRs.

(v) *Privately negotiated repurchases* (also called targeted repurchases):

Firms can repurchase shares directly from certain shareholders. In some of these cases, the repurchases are the result of activist or aggressive shareholders who threaten to acquire or meddle with the firm (thus, they are sometimes referred to as "green-mail," as a variation of the term "black-mail").

---

[1] In a fixed price tender offer, a firm might offer to repurchase one million shares at a price of $10. If a total of, say, 1.5 million shares are tendered, the proration factor will set at $1/1.5 = 67\%$, and this is the fraction of the shares that will be bought from the number of shares that were tendered by individual shareholders. In a Dutch auction, a firm might offer to repurchase one million shares at a price between $9 and $12. If 0.4 million shares are tendered at a price of $9, 0.6 million shares are tendered at $9.50, 0.5 million shares are tendered at $10, etc., the repurchase price will be set at $9.50, and all shares that were tendered at $9.50 or below will be bought at $9.50.

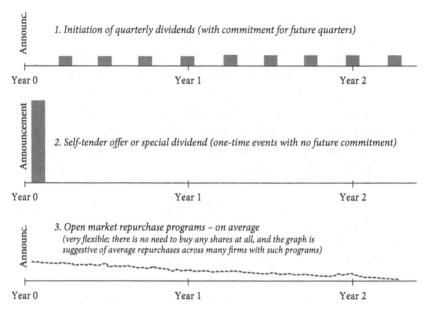

Figure 10.5 Typical payouts after announcements

Overall, the repurchase types differ primarily in the commitment/flexibility (with OMR programs offering the most flexibility) and the pace (with STOs, ASRs, and privately negotiated repurchases taking place in a shorter period than OMRs and preset repo plans).

The graphs in Figure 10.5 illustrate the differences in flexibility and pace for some payouts. Regular dividends are typically steady or modestly increasing over time. Self-tender offers and special dividends are large and occur over a short period. Finally, OMRs are flexible and typically occur over several years. But OMRs vary greatly (precisely due to their flexibility), and the graph is more indicative of the average repurchases across multiple repurchase programs than what individual cases might look like.

Figure 10.6 depicts possible implementations of hypothetical repurchase programs to emphasize their flexibility in both the timing and level of actual repurchases.

The graphs in Figure 10.7 show aggregate repurchases and dividends scaled by aggregate assets among public non-financial firms in each of the years from 1990 to 2020. In general, both dividends and repurchases increase with firm size. Furthermore, repurchases have increasingly represented a larger portion of total payouts in recent decades, and

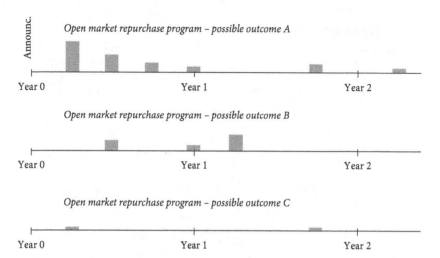

Figure 10.6 Examples of open market repurchase (OMR) programs

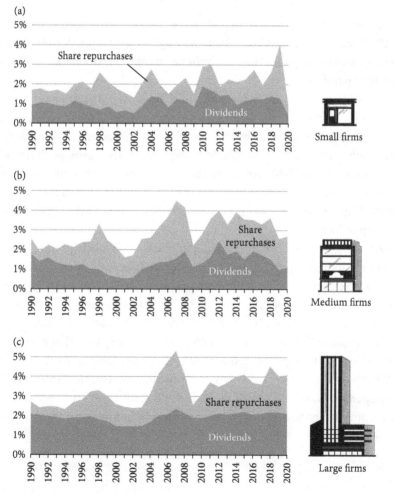

Figure 10.7 Payouts by firm size

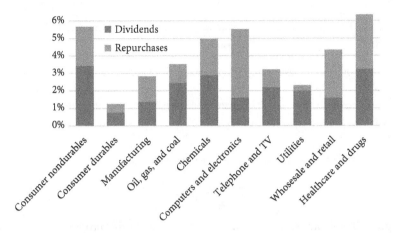

Figure 10.8 Payouts by industry

especially leading up to and including the first part of the financial crisis of 2007–8 for medium and large firms. Small firms had a notable increase in repurchases in 2019, but they cut both payment types dramatically during the 2020 pandemic.

Figure 10.8 shows the magnitudes of dividends and repurchases across industries. Firms in all sectors pay dividends and repurchase shares. Interestingly, the stable utility sector relies on the greatest proportion of dividends, with 87% of shareholder payouts in the form of dividends. Conversely, the unstable computer sector relies on the greatest proportion of repurchases, with 71% of shareholder payouts in the form of repurchases. We will later return to how uncertainty affects the choice between dividends and repurchases.

What about payouts to debtholders? Discussions of corporate payouts generally focus on payouts to shareholders, while payouts to debtholders are covered separately under the broader topic of capital structure policy. This book has a separate chapter on capital structure that discusses payouts to debtholders, because it is hard to have too many balls in the air at the same time. But I want to emphasize already now that payouts to debtholders can be considered a substitute for dividends and repurchases. All payouts reduce the cash balances available for investments and day-to-day operations, and several of them, including debt payments, serve as future commitments. Remain patient and we will jointly consider all payout choices later.

10.3 Tax treatment

The tax treatment of payouts can be complicated. The tax rates on dividends and capital gains have been similar in recent years. But capital gains are only taxed when the gains are realized (meaning that the shares are sold). On this basis, one could argue that firms should retain funds rather than disburse them to shareholders, and if shareholders need some liquidity, they can simply sell some shares. Indeed, some scholars have suggested that the popularity of dividends is puzzling.

What about the taxation of repurchases? In general, shareholders are taxed the same way when they sell shares back to the company as when they sell shares to other investors. That is, shareholders are taxed on any realized capital gains.[2]

Even if the tax rate on dividends and capital gains are the same, there are two reasons why the effective tax burden is typically substantially smaller for repurchases than for dividends:

- While the entire dividend is subject to taxation, only the part of a repurchase that represents a gain for shareholders who sell is subject to taxation. Chances are that the latter is much smaller than the former; in fact, the latter cannot be larger than the former, and it can even be negative if shareholders have experienced capital losses on the shares they sell.
- Shareholders can relatively easily offset any capital gains by realizing capital losses in their portfolio (i.e., sell some shares that have accumulated losses since purchase). The only prerequisite is that shareholders have a diversified portfolio of separate securities (i.e., not as part of a fund), such that they always have some securities with accumulated capital losses they can sell.[3]

Figure 10.9 illustrates the after-tax value of a $100 payout under different scenarios, assuming that the investor is in a medium tax bracket (i.e., income tax

---

[2] Starting January 1, 2023, corporations must also pay a 1% excise tax on repurchases.

[3] Incidentally, the same strategy of harvesting losses can be used to reduce your US taxable income by up to $3,000, allowing you to save about $1,000 on your annual taxes. To be able to do this every year, you must hold a diversified portfolio of individual stocks (not merely a diversified ETF), such that, at any time, some of the stocks have experienced capital gains and others have experienced losses. This gives you the flexibility to sell some of the stocks that have experienced losses up to $3,000. (Also, if you need to sell part of your portfolio for liquidity reasons, you can choose to sell a combination of shares that net out to have zero capital gains. But when netting losses and gains, be careful about how you mix those that are deemed to be "short-term" vs. "long-term.") If you were not aware of this, this book has more than paid for itself already.

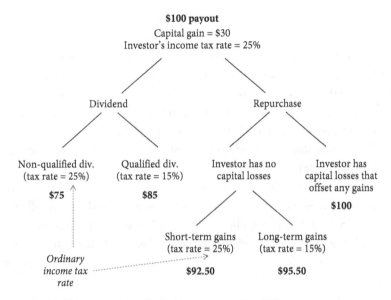

Figure 10.9 After-tax value of a $100 payout under different scenarios

rate is 25%) and 30% of the stock value comes from capital appreciation (e.g., the investor purchased the stock at $70 and it has since appreciated in value to $100). Based on these reasonable assumptions, we see that repurchases dominate dividends—even the lowest after-tax value on the repurchase side of $92.50 is higher than the highest after-tax value on the dividend side of $85.[4]

10.4 The primary payout motivation: Disburse excess cash

There are several possible reasons for firms to disburse cash to shareholders. The most obvious reason that follows from our earlier discussion is that firms have excess cash, meaning that the cash balance exceeds what is needed for the foreseeable future, perhaps as documented by simulations of future cash balances. As noted in Chapter 2, such excess cash might induce managers to spend lavishly or live an overly cushioned life, thus hurting shareholder value.

---

[4] Admittedly, the $100 after-tax value for repurchases where capital losses are used to offset losses is deceptively high, in that it does not consider that we used up some capital losses that we might otherwise have used to offset some other losses. But the effect is too small to change the main conclusion of this example.

However, not all firms with excess cash end up overinvesting in poor projects. The problem of overinvestment intensifies if the firms, in addition to excess cash, also:

- have poor corporate governance, including a weak corporate board, which ordinarily keeps management disciplined;
- lack promising investment opportunities in their core field of expertise; and
- operate in an industry with little competition, such that the firms can "afford" to slack.

Thus, firms that exhibit one or more of these characteristics have the most to gain from using payouts to remove excess cash.

An irony is that while firms with a combination of excess cash and poor governance can obtain great shareholder gains from payouts, their poor governance might make them unlikely to initiate such payouts. Think about it: Why would an undisciplined, power-hungry executive disburse cash holdings at her disposal, even if doing so benefits shareholders? The executive rather prefers to retain the cash as a cushion for a lavish lifestyle and to pursue pet projects, and the poor governance permits the executive to realize those preferences. I do not have a clear answer to this dilemma. But one possible solution resides in activist shareholders, who regularly identify firms that have the toxic combination of excess cash and poor governance and force them to either pay out excess cash or improve their governance.

Last, I should note that while payouts mitigate some problems by disciplining firms and its managers by removing excessive organizational slack, they could also create some problems. In particular, aggressive payout policies that commit firms to high payouts for an extended period could cause cash shortages in the future. Thus, payout decisions should consider the entire cash distribution, including the left and the right tails, and capture the effect that payouts have on the distribution. In that way, payout policy differs from risk management, which focuses on the left tail of the cash distribution.

10.5 Other payout motivations

Even though I believe that the primary reason for payouts is to disburse excess cash, it is useful to briefly discuss other payout motivations. But you will see that even some of those alternate motivations are tied to firms' cash levels.

Cater to investor preferences

Different investors have different payout preferences:

o Some investors prefer that companies retain their funds, such that the investors get their return in the form of capital gains that they can defer for tax purposes.
o Some investors prefer that companies pay dividends, perhaps because this provides investors with "current income" or because such companies are perceived to be safer.[5]
o Some investors prefer that companies repurchase shares, perhaps because of the favorable tax treatment relative to dividends.

If one of the investor types dominates the shareholder group, the company might adopt a policy that reflects the preferences of these investors. Investors might even communicate their preferences to the firm, either privately or publicly.

Related to the notion that investors have certain preferences, it is also likely that aggregate preferences change over time. For example, in turbulent times, investors might flock toward dividend-paying stocks, because such stocks are perceived to be safer. Firms might, in turn, cater to such time-varying preferences in an effort to boost the demand for the stock and the stock price. For example, if there is substantial demand for dividend-paying stocks, firms might raise dividends to meet that demand.

Deter takeovers

Firms occasionally use payouts to defend against hostile takeover attempts. There are several reasons why payouts effectively deter takeovers. For example, they reduce the cash balance that might have motivated the suitor to target the company in the first place. Another example is that repurchases remove shareholders who are most willing to sell their shares, such that the

---

[5] I do believe that dividend-paying stocks are generally safer, but not *because* of their dividends. Be careful with cause and effect here. Suppose you walk through a neighborhood with nicely manicured gardens. You would probably conclude that the neighborhood is safe, right? But it is not the manicured gardens that make the neighborhood safe; rather, the gardens are indicative of the resources and preferences in the neighborhood that make it safe. In any event, if you are looking for safe stocks, there are better measures of risk than dividends, including beta and stock return volatility.

suitor must pay a higher price to persuade remaining shareholders to sell enough shares to obtain the majority required to complete the acquisition.

Inflate earnings per share (EPS)

Firms sometimes state that they undertake repurchases to increase the EPS. However, whether repurchases actually raise the EPS and whether raising EPS contributes to a higher stock price are both unclear. First, while repurchases reduce the number of shares, they also reduce the earnings because of the lost earnings from the funds used to buy shares or because of increased interest expenses from new debt used to finance the repurchases. Second, even if EPS increases, it is likely that (a) the cost of equity increases due to the increased debt ratio and (b) the growth in future EPS decreases. The net effect on the stock price is unclear. Thus, I would never focus on the short-term effect on EPS when deciding whether to repurchase shares.

Exploit undervaluation

If managers believe that their firms' shares are undervalued, they could exploit the undervaluation by repurchasing shares. Indeed, firms often state that their shares are undervalued when they announce repurchases. One might counter that managers always seem to claim that their firm's shares are undervalued, perhaps because managers are overconfident or because they attempt to jack up the price, and that such claims should be taken with a grain of salt. But in a repurchase, managers at least "put their feet where their mouths are," such that repurchases are more credible indications of undervaluation than mere statements of undervaluation.

Signal firm prospects

Increases in payouts are generally viewed as good news, as evidenced by stock price increases upon announcements of payout increases. This is consistent with firms undertaking a simulation suggesting that future cash balances are sufficiently strong to warrant payout increases. Consider the illustration in Figure 10.10. The insiders of the firm know whether the prospects are good or poor. If the prospects are good, the projected future cash distribution

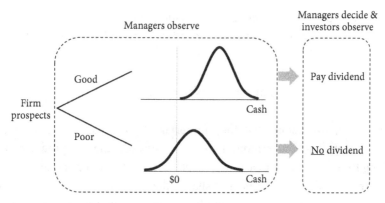

Figure 10.10 Dividend signaling

is strong, and the firm will pay a dividend. If the prospects are poor, the projected cash distribution is weak, and the firm will not pay a dividend. If investors are unable to directly gauge whether firm prospects are good or poor, they can nevertheless infer the prospects from the dividend decisions. In that sense, payouts *signal* what insiders think about future prospects to outside investors.

But some scholars have taken this a step further. They conjecture that managers use payouts as a deliberate signaling tool to raise stock prices. The counterargument to this is that, while payout increases do indeed raise stock prices, the stock prices would eventually increase anyway as the good news about future prospects find its way to the capital market. The only way such a *deliberate* signal would make sense is that the firm or its insiders have an imminent need to sell shares. But if the firm needs to raise funds, would it make sense to increase payouts? I do not think so. So while payout increases signal good news, I do not think signaling is a major motivation. That is, I think that the signal from payout increases is mostly *unintentional*. Similarly, you might have a nice car, which conveys that you have some wealth, but it might not have been your intention to signal or boast that wealth when you bought the car. (Ok—I admit that for some people it probably is, but you get my point.)

In summary, I believe that payout reasons beyond the desire to disburse cash are secondary. Even firms that, say, cater to investor demand for payouts or have the need to fight off takeover attempts, should first consider if they have sufficient cash to undertake payouts.

10.6 The choice of payout type: The effect of cash levels and flow

As stated earlier, I believe that the primary reason for payouts is to disburse cash. Which payout type disburses cash most effectively depends on the level and stability of the firm's current and expected future cash.

Recall that:

- STOs and special dividends are one-time transactions and generally very large transactions,
- OMRs offer great flexibility with regard to both timing and completion, and
- regular (quarterly) dividends are very sticky, in the sense that they are rarely reduced.

There are several implications from these features.

- If a firm experiences a cash flow spike, e.g., from the sale of an asset, a share repurchase or special dividend can be used to disburse that cash with no future payout commitments.
- If a firm exhibits strong cash flow that routinely accumulates as excess cash, i.e., the firm is essentially what some refer to as a "cash cow," a regular dividend can be used to offset the cash flow now and in the future.

Let us consider some examples based on simulated cash levels over the next three years. The goal is to bring the cash level down as much as possible, but still not have a chance of a shortage.

In the first example in Figure 10.11, a firm has a current cash balance of $100, and the cash balance is expected to increase modestly during the next years. The shaded area shows the 90% confidence interval for the cash distribution, and it suggests a modest standard deviation. In short, the firm appears to have excess cash, primarily because of the high current cash level and the low uncertainty, and not because of a particularly strong cash flow. I have considered three payout strategies:

(i) increase the annual dividend by $20 (if the dividends are paid quarterly, it would be an increase of quarterly dividends of $5),
(ii) an $80 STO, or

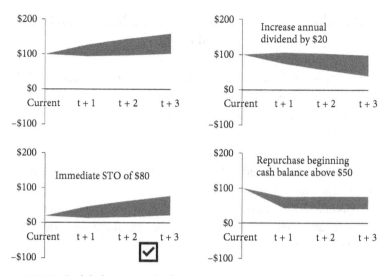

Figure 10.11 Cash balances under four payout strategies—example 1

    (iii) an OMR program that entails using cash balances in excess of $50 at the beginning of the year on repurchases.

All payout strategies reduce the cash balance substantially without endangering future liquidity. But the regular dividend increase works rather slowly, in that it takes a couple of years before the cash level comes down meaningfully. I am also a bit worried about the dividend commitment in years beyond $t + 3$. In my opinion, the STO works best here, because it quickly gets rid of substantial cash, and the future cash levels are low but not in danger of being negative.

The second example in Figure 10.12 is similar to the first, except that the standard deviation of future cash levels is much higher. Given the higher standard deviation, a regular dividend increase is not appealing. As a rule of thumb, high cash flow uncertainty combined with the commitment of a regular dividend is a recipe for disaster in the long run—so do not try this at home, kids. We further see that the STO is too aggressive, leaving a large chance of cash shortages in the future. The most suitable strategy here is to initiate the OMR program, because it allows the flexibility to abstain from repurchasing if the cash level is low. One could argue, however, that even the suggested OMR program is too aggressive and should be scaled back to, e.g., repurchasing beginning cash balances above $60.

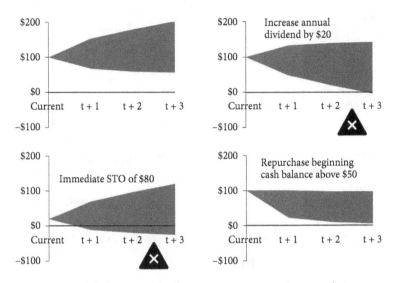

Figure 10.12 Cash balances under four payout strategies—example 2

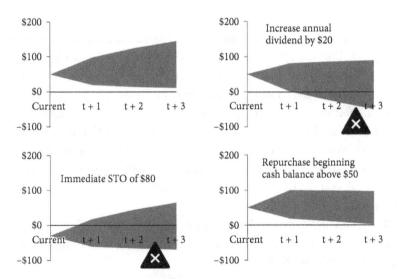

Figure 10.13 Cash balances under four payout strategies—example 3

The third example in Figure 10.13 is similar to the second example, with the exception that the current cash balance is only $50. In that case, the STO is clearly a bad choice, as the cash balance immediately turns negative. The regular dividend is also detrimental, though it will take longer to see the negative consequences. This firm probably might not need a payout at all. But if

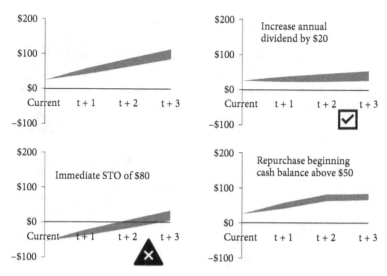

Figure 10.14 Cash balances under four payout strategies—example 4

it chooses to disburse funds, it should only do so if the cash flow is unexpect-edly good. The OMR program affords that flexibility, which is why the graph shows the probability of a cash shortage is barely higher under the OMR pro-gram than under the strategy of not disbursing funds.

In the fourth example in Figure 10.14, the current cash balance is lower yet at $25, but the cash flow is strong and steady, such that the future cash balance is likely to grow substantially. In that case, the commitment of a con-tinuous dividend makes much more sense than in the previous examples. We further see that the OMR program works even here. In contrast, the STO is clearly unsuitable for this firm.

The graphs in Figure 10.15, which depict the time-series of net income and payouts scaled by assets for four major firms, provide further insight on the use of dividends and repurchases.

- The dividends are fairly stable for all firms, with some exceptions:
  o Caterpillar reduced the dividends in the early 1980s and again in the early 1990s, each time after large losses.
  o IBM steadily reduced the dividends in the 1980s, and more dramati-cally in the early 1990s after consecutive losses.

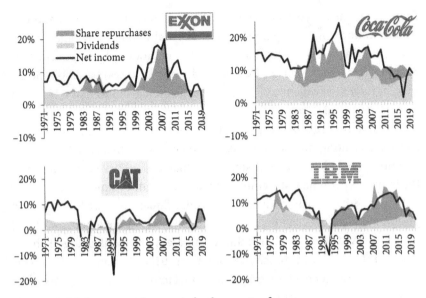

Figure 10.15 Income and payouts for four major firms

- The two firms with the strongest and least volatile net income, Exxon and Coca-Cola, have paid the largest dividends.
- Repurchases were more common in recent decades. But they fluctuate greatly, following the pattern of net income quite closely.

Overall, the graphs suggest that firms pay dividends when they have strong and persistent earnings, and supplement with repurchases for the portion of earnings that is more volatile and temporary.

10.7 The payout choice: The case of Herbalife

Herbalife Nutrition Ltd. develops and sells a variety of nutrition and weight-management products, including meal-replacement shake powder, protein shakes, and vitamins. Herbalife is a so-called multi-level marketer (MLM) and distributes its products through a direct selling business model, which the 2017 Annual Report describes this way: "Many individuals become part of our direct selling network simply to buy products at a discount directly from us for their own consumption. Others choose to also retail and distribute products that they purchase from us. Finally, some individuals choose to also build a direct sales force and earn compensation (which could include commissions, royalty overrides, and production bonuses) based on the activity of their sales organizations, as well as an annual bonus that is based on several additional factors."

Herbalife rewards its independent contractors both for selling products and for recruiting others to do so. The danger with this structure is that recruiting might become more important than product sales, in which case the result is a pyramidal structure, just like chain-letter scams.

In 2012, Bill Ackman's hedge fund, Pershing Square, took a $1 billion short position in Herbalife, calling it a pyramid scheme. On the other side of that bet was activist investor Carl Icahn, who became Herbalife's largest shareholder at about the same time.[6] In February of 2018, Ackman closed his short position after losses of close to $1 billion (including losses on put options he acquired at the end of 2017).

Figure 10.16 shows the stock performance of Herbalife from 2012 until the first part of 2018. While the stock price was quite volatile during this period, its overall performance was about on par with S&P 500 due to a strong run-up in January and February of 2018.

Figure 10.17 shows selected items from the financial statements. Herbalife enjoyed a pretty stable net operating income from 2012 through 2017, with

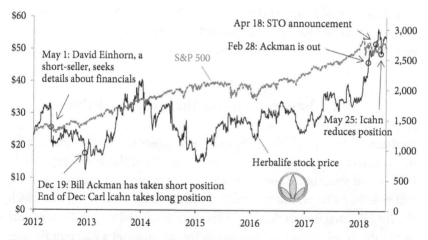

Figure 10.16 The stock price of Herbalife

---

[6] The 2016 documentary "Betting on Zero" is an entertaining and informative recount of events.

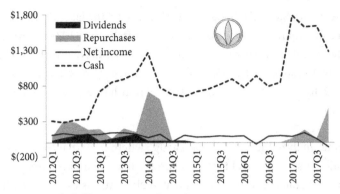

Figure 10.17 Herbalife's income, cash, and payouts

the exception of a few sporadic dips, including one during the last quarter of 2017. Meanwhile, the cash balance accumulated substantially, and it had about $1.3 billion in cash at the end of 2017.[7] The company paid regular dividends through 2014 but announced on April 28, 2014, that it would terminate its dividend and use the cash to repurchase shares instead. On February 21, 2017, Herbalife announced a new three-year $1.5 billion open market repurchase (OMR) program, and the graph shows that it spent almost $800 million on share repurchases in 2017. Thus, it still had $700 million left of its program at the beginning of 2018 and could naturally expand the program if it wished.

On this backdrop, what should the company do with its payouts? Should it reintroduce regular dividends? Should it continue with its periodic repurchases via the OMR program? Or should it undertake a self-tender offer (STO)?

Before we proceed with our analysis, I can reveal that Herbalife announced an STO on April 18, 2018:

> Herbalife Ltd. (NYSE: HLF) ("Herbalife" or "the Company") announced today it has commenced a "modified Dutch auction" self-tender offer to purchase in cash up to an aggregate $600 million of shares of its common stock at a per share price not greater than $108.00 nor less than $98.00 (the "tender offer"). The closing price of Herbalife's common shares on

---

[7] The dramatic increase in cash in the first quarter of 2017 was due to a new $1,450 million senior secured credit facility, consisting of a $1,300 million term loan and a $150 million revolving credit facility.

the New York Stock Exchange on April 17, 2018, the last full trading day before the commencement of the tender offer, was $103.02 per share. The tender offer is scheduled to expire at 5:00 P.M., New York City time, on May 16, 2018, unless the offer is extended. (Considering a subsequent 2-for-1 stock split, the Dutch auction had a price range of $49 to $54.)

Now, let us analyze the situation and gauge whether Herbalife's course of action made sense. To do so, I first made pro forma statements based on historical financial statements and then created simulations of future cash levels using Crystal Ball. You will also notice a line for payouts, which I initially set to zero for each of the future years.[8]

Herbalife lists several risk factors in its 2017 Annual Report, including the following:

- The failure to establish and maintain member and sales leader relationships.
- Adverse publicity associated with its products or network marketing program.
- Stricter regulation of multi-level marketers (MLMs).

These risk factors undoubtedly contribute to the uncertainty of revenues. I have embedded this uncertainty in the standard deviation of revenue growth of 5%. Thus, with an expected growth rate of 1%, the 95% confidence interval for future growth is roughly –9% to 11%. I will not discuss my other assumptions, but rather just state them in the spreadsheet. The two "Simulation" columns contain the hidden distribution assumptions (and are therefore colored green) and display the assumed means of the distributions by default. The two "Std deviation" columns display the assumed standard deviations of the distributions.

---

[8] While the accounting for dividends and repurchases differ, I do not separate how the various payout strategies are accounted for in my balance sheets, because the effect on the cash holdings is not affected. In particular, irrespective of the payout type, I simply reduce the equity in the balance sheet by the dollar value of the payout.

	2016	2017	2018E	2019E	Simulation 2018E	Simulation 2019E	Std deviation 2018E	Std deviation 2019E	
Net sales	$4,488	$4,428	$4,472	$4,517	1%	1%	5.0%	5.0%	Growth
Cost of sales	$855	$849	$850	$858	19%	19%	1.0%	1.0%	Fraction of sales
Gross profit	$3,634	$3,579	$3,622	$3,659					
Royalty overrides	$1,273	$1,254	$1,252	$1,265	28%	28%	1.0%	1.0%	Fraction of sales
SG&A expenses	$1,967	$1,759	$1,834	$1,852	41%	41%	2.0%	2.0%	Fraction of sales
Other operating income	$(64)	$(51)	$(22)	$(23)	−0.5%	−0.5%	0.5%	0.5%	Fraction of sales
Operating income	$458	$617	$559	$565					
Interest expense	$99	$161	$217	$206	10% of beginning long-term debt				
Interest income	$6	$15	$17	$26	2% of beginning cash				
Income before taxes	$365	$471	$359	$384					
Income taxes	$105	$257	$90	$96	25%	25%	2.0%	2.0%	
Net income	$260	$214	$269	$288					
Payout			$0	$0					
Cash and equiv.	$844	$1,279	$1,378	$1,557	PLUG				
Receivables	$70	$93	$89	$90	2%	2%	0.5%	0.5%	Fraction of sales
Inventories	$371	$341	$358	$361	8%	8%	1.0%	1.0%	Fraction of sales
Prepaid expenses	$177	$147	$157	$158	3.5%	3.5%	0.5%	0.5%	Fraction of sales
Total current assets	$1,463	$1,860	$1,981	$2,167					
PP&E	$378	$378	$383	$389	1.5%	1.5%	0.5%	0.5%	Growth

	2016	2017	2018E	2019E	Simulation 2018E	Simulation 2019E	Std deviation 2018E	Std deviation 2019E	
Intangible assets	$310	$310	$310	$310					
Goodwill	$90	$97	$99	$101	2%	2%	1.0%	1.0%	Growth
Other assets	$325	$250	$253	$255	1%	1%	2.0%	2.0%	Growth
Total assets	$2,565	$2,895	$3,026	$3,222					
Accounts payable	$66	$68	$68	$69	8%	8%	0.5%	0.5%	Fr. of cost of sales
Royalty overrides	$261	$278	$263	$266	21%	21%	1.0%	1.0%	Fr. of roy. ov. in IS
Current portion of LT debt	$10	$102	$100	$100					
Other current liabil.	$455	$459	$447	$452	10%	10%	1.0%	1.0%	Fraction of sales
Total current liabil.	$792	$907	$878	$886					
Long-term debt	$1,438	$2,166	$2,063	$1,963	Assuming $100 is paid off each year and no new debt				
Other non-current liabilities	$139	$157	$150	$150					
Total liabilities	$2,369	$3,230	$3,091	$2,999					
Equity	$196	$(335)	$(65)	$223					
Total liabilities and equity	$2,565	$2,895	$3,026	$3,222					

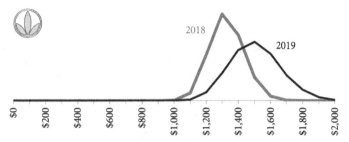

Figure 10.18 Simulated cash distributions for Herbalife with no payout

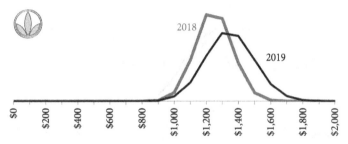

Figure 10.19 Simulated cash distributions for Herbalife with $80 million annual dividends

Figure 10.18 shows that the simulated cash levels for the next couple of years are high, ranging between one and two billion dollars and with no chance of a cash shortage. If my assumptions are reasonable, the company can readily afford to disburse some cash.

Then I introduced alternative payout strategies. First, I introduced an $80 million annual dividend, which corresponds to a dividend yield of roughly 2% (a bit above the average dividend yield among large firms). As Figure 10.19 indicates, the dividends slowly deplete the cash levels. But because (a) the firm currently has so much cash, (b) the cash flow is expected to be positive, and (c) the dividend effect is so gradual, I view a dividend to be insufficient in this case.

Next, I introduce an STO of $600 million, which is what the firm actually announced. Figure 10.20 shows that the cash level drops immediately by about $600 million, and future cash levels drop a little more.[9] Incidentally,

[9] The cash levels decrease by a little more than $600 million, because I have assumed that keeping the cash internally would have generated some interest income.

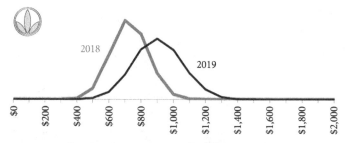

Figure 10.20 Simulated cash distributions for Herbalife with $600 million STO

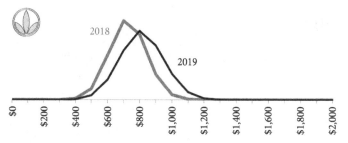

Figure 10.21 Simulated cash distributions for Herbalife with STO and OMR

a special dividend would have the same effect for the company. Despite the substantial drop in cash level, there is still no chance of a cash shortage.

Last, I combine the STO with a flexible OMR program, where any cash in excess of $700 million at the beginning of 2019 is spent on repurchases.[10] Not surprisingly, Figure 10.21 shows that this strategy lowers the cash distribution for 2019 further and yields a narrower distribution.

In my opinion, the last strategy of an STO combined with a flexible OMR is a suitable alternative for Herbalife. The strategy puts a substantial dent in the cash holdings of Herbalife, while not risking any cash shortage in the next couple of years. One might also argue that the OMR should be even more aggressive.

Incidentally, Herbalife completed the STO. The offer was oversubscribed, and the company repurchased 11.4 million shares (representing 6.5% of shares outstanding) at a price of $52.50 for a total cost of roughly $600 million.[11]

---

[10] To implement this, I state that the payout in 2019 equals MAX(0, Cash balance at the end of 2018 – 700). Incidentally, the expected repurchase in 2019 under this strategy is $93 million.

[11] Carl Icahn sold 10.5 million Herbalife shares valued at approximately $550 million in the tender offer.

10.8 The choice to cut payouts: The case of General Electric

Another payout event that received substantial media attention was GE's announcement on October 30, 2018, to cut its dividend from $0.12 to only a penny. At the same time, it announced the dreadful quarterly EPS of –$2.63. I will not develop a full analysis for this case; rather, I will use some simple numbers and trends to paint a picture.

GE is a multinational company that operates in many sectors, including aviation, power, renewable energy, healthcare, and capital. At its peak, it was the most valuable company in the United States, with a value of more than half a trillion in August 2000. Furthermore, with almost 10 billion shares outstanding, it was among the most widely owned stocks.[12]

But during the last couple of decades, GE's performance has weakened, and its dividend payouts have been erratic. Figure 10.22 shows the historical EPS and dividends per share, and Figure 10.23 shows the historical stock price performance. The quarterly dividend plunged from $0.41 in the first quarter of 2000 to $0.14 in the second quarter the same year. Then it gradually increased to $0.31 in 2008 but dropped again in the third quarter of 2009 to $0.10. Then, yet again, it gradually increased, this time to $0.24 in 2017,

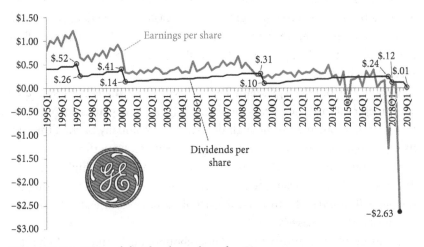

Figure 10.22 EPS and dividend per share for GE

---

[12] Think about what that means for the cash flow if, say, the quarterly dividend was $0.40 (and the annual dividend was $1.60).

Figure 10.23 Stock price performance of GE

but was cut in half to $0.12 in the first quarter of 2018. And, then, finally, it was cut to a penny by 2019.

The EPS (a driver of the cash flow) helps explain what happened. Figure 10.22 shows that the EPS easily exceeded the dividend per share from 1995 through 2008. But with declines in EPS, especially in the first quarters of 1997 and 2000, GE implemented dramatic dividend cuts to keep the dividends comfortably below the EPS. With reasonably stable EPS in the beginning of the current century, GE management must have felt comfortable in gradually increasing the dividend. But when the EPS dipped below the dividend in 2009, it cut the dividend by two-thirds. Nevertheless, the management returned to its habit of gradually increasing the dividend, a decision that should have been questioned. Wasn't it time to switch to a more flexible payout method then? Could GE really sustain the policy of gradually increasing the dividend again?

Well, the payout strategy seemed to have backfired when the EPS suffered some major hits just a few years thereafter. With several quarters of poor performance combined with the high dividend, the company burned through its cash balance. Did the management group expect the performance to rebound soon? How could they otherwise keep on paying the high dividend? This might just be an example of how reluctant managers are to cutting the dividend. It would certainly make them look stupid to cut the dividends after the substantial increases since 2010.

In any event, the performance did not rebound much, and in 2017 it actually got worse, forcing the company to throw in the towel by cutting the dividend in half. Given the continued poor performance, it was not surprising that it essentially omitted the dividend altogether the year thereafter. Many outsiders, recognizing that the dividend was unsustainable, expected this decision.

It is easy to look at this with perfect hindsight and criticize GE's payout decisions. Nevertheless, I cannot resist. In my opinion, the company was far too aggressive in its dividend payouts. Despite several setbacks, the company kept pumping up the dividend. In my mind, the company should have chosen to switch to repurchases years ago. When it instead chose to continue to pay high dividends, it was eventually left with no choice but to essentially omit the dividends (a "painful but necessary" step according to Larry Culp, who became the CEO less than a one month before the omission).[13] In short, GE appears to have violated our principle of only raising dividends when a careful analysis of future liquidity shows that the company can sustain it.

10.9 The choice of payout type: The effect of undervaluation and taxation

Both the valuation (or rather "mispricing") of shares and taxation are also relevant factors in the choice between dividends and repurchases.

If managers believe that the capital market currently undervalues the firm's equity, it makes more sense to disburse cash via share repurchases than via dividends, and vice versa. In fact, I even mentioned this as a possible motivation for repurchasing shares in the first place. There are, however, a couple of limitations to this argument.

- If the repurchase takes the form of an STO, the repurchase generally takes place at a significant premium above the pre-announcement stock price. Thus, STOs are not ideal for exploiting undervaluation.
- Philosophically, it is questionable whether managers should exploit undervaluation by repurchasing shares. Repurchasing undervalued shares effectively transfers wealth from shareholders who sell to those who do not sell. But such discrimination is inconsistent with managers working for *all current* shareholders.

---

[13] With about 8.6 billion shares in 2018, the quarterly dividend of $0.24 cost would have cost about $8 billion annually.

Thus, to the extent that managers seek to exploit undervaluation via share repurchases, they should probably do so by repurchasing the shares in the open market and realize that this is effectively a zero-sum game that benefits long-term shareholders at the expense of shareholders who sell.

I already discussed the differential taxation of dividends and share repurchases. I noted that repurchases generally impose a smaller tax burden on shareholders than do dividends. But how much smaller the tax burden is depends on (i) the relative tax rates on dividends and capital gains, (ii) the basis prices of shareholders (i.e., what they paid for the shares and, therefore, their cumulative capital gain), and (iii) the extent to which shareholders can neutralize realized capital gains with other transactions. The implication for managers choosing between payouts and repurchases is that the following observable factors matter:

- Share price run-up: Firms that have experienced small capital gains (or even losses) should repurchase shares.
- Dividend yield: Firms with a history of paying large dividends have probably attracted investor clienteles that like dividends, perhaps because they face a low tax rate on dividends. Thus, repurchases are somewhat less appealing for those firms.
- Prevailing tax rates on dividends and capital gains: Obviously, as the tax rate on dividends relative to the tax rate on capital gains increases, repurchases are relatively more appealing. Indeed, the earlier graph of quarterly and special dividends showed an increase in special dividends in response to the dividend tax cut in 2003.

But, again, I want to underscore that repurchases generally dominate dividends for tax purposes; the only question is the magnitude of this dominance.

10.10 Bringing it all together into a payout matrix

I have emphasized the type of cash level and cash flow as the main determinant of both whether to pay out cash and what payout method is most suitable, and undervaluation and taxation as additional factors in the choice of payout method. I have combined all factors into the payout matrix in Figure 10.24 that organizes these ideas. But there is an open space in the matrix, and we will work on filling that in the next chapter.

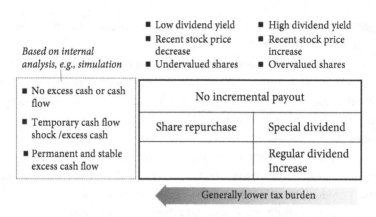

Based on internal analysis, e.g., simulation	■ Low dividend yield ■ Recent stock price decrease ■ Undervalued shares	■ High dividend yield ■ Recent stock price increase ■ Overvalued shares
■ No excess cash or cash flow	No incremental payout	
■ Temporary cash flow shock /excess cash	Share repurchase	Special dividend
■ Permanent and stable excess cash flow		Regular dividend Increase

Generally lower tax burden

Figure 10.24 Payout matrix

10.11 A case study of Apple

I will finish the chapter with a highly public case study of activist investor Carl Icahn's effort to pressure Apple Inc. to disburse cash. At the end of the fiscal year 2013 (September 30, 2013), Apple had $147 billion in cash and cash equivalents, of which $106 billion was in long-term marketable securities. Furthermore, $111 billion of the cash and cash equivalents (about 76%) was held in foreign subsidiaries and subject to US income taxation on repatriation to the United States.[14] This cash hoard, enough to buy either Citigroup Inc. or Bank of America Corp., triggered public outcry and shareholder activism. In late 2013, Carl Icahn demanded that the company repurchase more shares. I have outlined the major events and the back-and-forth arguments of Apple and Icahn below.

There is no doubt that Apple had excessive cash at the end of 2013; despite a volatile industry and the need for high R&D and periodic acquisitions, there was no chance that Apple would run out of cash in the next several years. However, the tricky thing about this case is that most of the cash was held in subsidiaries overseas. If Apple wanted to disburse this cash to its shareholders, it would first have to transfer the cash to the parent company, which would trigger substantial repatriation taxes. Rather than facing the repatriation tax, Apple had several choices, including (1) hire some clever tax

---

[14] The cash held by foreign subsidiaries was not necessarily deposited in banks overseas and invested in securities overseas. Rather, much of this cash, perhaps even most of it, was deposited in US banks and invested in US securities.

lawyers who might find some tax loophole, (2) invest the cash overseas, or (3) wait for a tax holiday.

How should we think about the overseas cash then? While it might be too expensive for the parent company to tap into this cash as a source of liquidity, it could be used as "collateral" for a loan. That is, a parent company should be able to borrow very cheaply, because, in the worst-case scenario, the overseas cash can be brought back to the United States to pay off the loan. The parent company could then use the proceeds from the loan to disburse cash to shareholders. But if Apple were to be forced to bring the cash back to the United States, it would come at a cost (i.e., the repatriation tax) that is akin to the cost of raising equity in the capital market. In that sense, the repatriation tax is just another ripple effect that kicks in once Apple runs out of domestic cash.

What do you think?

Incidentally, Figure 10.25 shows that Apple bumped up the payouts to shareholders to more than $50 billion in each of the fiscal years 2014 and 2015, and most of this came in the form of repurchases. Thus, the cash level at the parent dwindled from about $35 billion at the end of FY2013 to about $18 billion at the end of both FY2014 and FY2015. But Apple's overseas operations continued to generate lots of cash such that the overall cash level increased, and the fraction of overall cash that was overseas increased from 76% at the end of FY2013 to about 90% at the end of both FY2104 and FY2015.

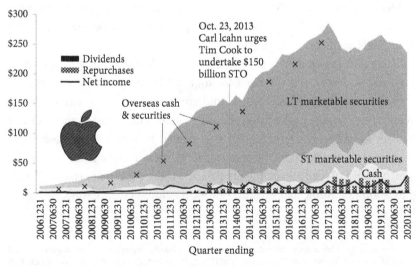

Figure 10.25 Income, cash, and payouts for Apple

- *Icahn's Letter to Tim Cook—October 23, 2013*
  Carl Icahn, who owned $2.5 billion worth of Apple shares, argued that Apple's stock was greatly undervalued and noted that Apple held $147 billion in cash and was expected to generate $51 billion in EBIT the following year. Thus, Icahn urged Apple to undertake a $150 billion self-tender offer.
- *Apple's Response to Icahn's Letter*
  Apple responded that it was reviewing and seeking shareholder input on its share repurchase policy and would announce any changes to its policy in the first part of 2014.
- *Icahn Filed Apple Shareholder Proposal—November 26, 2013*
  Icahn filed a shareholder proposal calling for an expansion of Apple's share repurchase program. The proposal was precatory, meaning that if the majority of Apple shareholders approved, it would be non-binding on Apple's management.
- *Apple's Response to Icahn's Shareholder Proposal—December 4, 2013*
  Apple stated that it regularly reviews and seeks shareholders' input on its shareholder payout policy, and that the board and management have been in an ongoing discussion regarding shareholder payout policy since October.
- *Apple's Response to Icahn's Shareholder Proposal—December 27, 2013*
  Apple's management and board issued a statement recommending shareholders to reject Icahn's share repurchase proposal. They argued that such a rejection would preserve necessary financial flexibility and avoid repatriation taxes associated with bringing back cash from overseas.
- *Icahn's Letter to Apple Shareholders—January 24, 2014*
  Icahn found Apple's argument to be irrational, claiming Apple was vastly overcapitalized. He contended that Apple's remaining cash hoard after the implementation of his proposal would be enough for acquisitions and R&D, and that Apple would not have to bring back cash from overseas.
- *Icahn's Letter to Apple Shareholders—February 10, 2014*
  Icahn dropped his non-binding share repurchase proposal before the shareholder meeting on February 28. Icahn's decision was influenced by Institutional Shareholder Services' recommendation to vote against the proposal. In addition, Apple was on track to repurchase $32 billion in shares for fiscal 2014, which Icahn believed was satisfactory.

Antony Filippo, an independent investment manager, summarized it as follows: "It looks like Icahn's crusade paid off. Apple's board and Icahn are meeting halfway."

- *Apple's Response to Icahn's Letter—April 23, 2014*
  Apple reported strong earnings and announced a stock split and a payout increase. Apple's CFO Peter Oppenheimer explained that Apple "generated $13.5 billion in cash flow from operations and returned almost $21 billion in cash to shareholders through dividends and share repurchases during the March quarter."

- *Icahn's Letter to Tim Cook—October 9, 2014*
  Icahn, now owning $5.3 billion of Apple stock, again urged Apple to make a self-tender offer "to accelerate and increase the magnitude of share repurchases."

- *Apple's Response to Icahn's Letter*
  Apple stated that it must consider input from all shareholders and that it reviews the share repurchase program annually. It further described how it has executed the largest capital return program in corporate history since 2013; it had already returned $74 billion to shareholders and planned to return $130 billion by the following year.

11

Debt Payouts and Capital Structure

11.1 Debt payouts: Commitment and default

When firms borrow money, they are contractually obligated to pay it back with interest. The contractual obligations create a commitment that is much stronger than payouts to shareholders. We can view the various payouts to shareholders and debtholders on a continuum with different commitment levels, as Figure 11.1 illustrates.

If the firm is unable to fulfill its debt payment obligations, the firm will default. Figure 11.2 shows one perspective of default, in which default occurs when the total asset value falls below the value of total liabilities. This is same framework that we discussed earlier under structural models for estimating the probability of default. A key insight to this framework is that default only occurs with debt. Without debt, the worst that can happen is that the firm runs out of cash, and we are back to the ripple effects discussed earlier in the book.

A shortcoming of the graph is that firms do not necessarily default when the value falls below the debt value; as long as the firm still has cash to pay its ongoing debt payments, it might dodge default. This suggests that retaining cash can be even more critical when firms have looming debt payments.

Another shortcoming of the graph is that it fails to convey that debt covenants (e.g., requirements to maintain various financial ratios) might be violated before the firm defaults. In the case of a covenant violation, the lender could, for example, call the loan, increase the interest rate, or increase the collateral, all of which would impose additional costs for the borrower.

Importantly, default can produce much greater ripple effects than mere cash shortages. Not only will the firm have to forgo investment opportunities and scale back operations, it will also have to restructure the debt. And while raising funds when the firm is short on cash can be challenging and expensive, it is almost impossible for a firm that has defaulted.

The example in Figure 11.3 illustrates how the debt commitments can choke a firm. Suppose a company's face value of debt is $1 billion, and the

Applied Corporate Risk and Liquidity Management. Erik Lie, Oxford University Press. © Oxford University Press 2023.
DOI: 10.1093/oso/9780197664995.003.0011

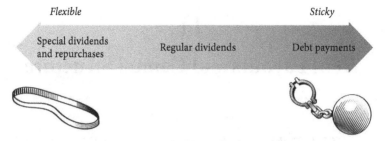

Figure 11.1 Commitment levels of payouts to shareholders and debtholders

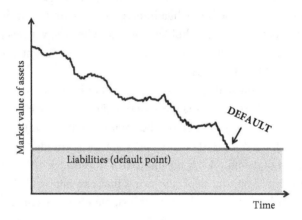

Figure 11.2 Debt default

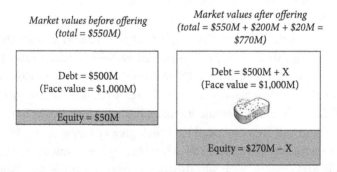

Figure 11.3 Example of debt overhang

market values of debt and equity are $500 million and $50 million, respectively. Further, suppose that an equity issue of $200 million would allow the firm to invest in a project with NPV of $20 million, thus raising the market value of the company to $770 million ($550 million + $200 million + $20 million). The equity issue would also inflate the market value of debt by $X million, that is, there would be an immediate wealth transfer of $X million from equityholders to debtholders. Given the equity infusion and the NPV, X would have to be somewhere between $0 and $220 million, and most likely it will exceed $100 million. It is as if the old debt works as a sponge, sucking up most of the new value. If X is $100 million (which is likely conservative), the new equity value is $170 million. And what investor would willingly invest $200 million to get part of $170 million? Thus, despite the positive NPV, the equity issue is infeasible due to the large *debt overhang*.

The firm could attempt to restructure the debt obligations when it is in default or when default is imminent. But a *private workout* with creditors is difficult, if not impossible, because creditors who choose not to participate in the restructuring might strengthen their position relative to other creditors, giving rise to *holdout problems*.

Suppose that the firm with debt overhang attempts to undertake an equity-for-debt exchange offer, but that a debtholder representing 10% of the debt chooses not to participate, that is, the debtholder chooses to "hold out." This is shown in Figure 11.4. The creditor who holds out increases the market value of her debt from 10% × $500M = $50M to $100; the creditors who accept equity decrease the market value of their securities from .9 × $500M = $450M to q × $470, where q = <0,1>. Clearly, the creditor who holds out is better off, but it is doubtful whether other creditors are. This holdout problem is particularly severe if there are many creditors, if the firm is in deep distress, and if the restructuring fails to recoup much value.

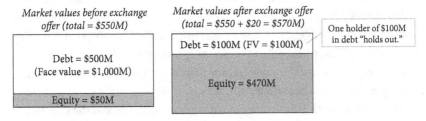

Figure 11.4 Example of holdout in exchange offer

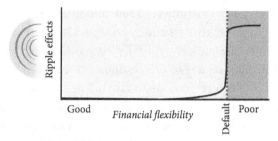

Figure 11.5 The surging ripple effects around default

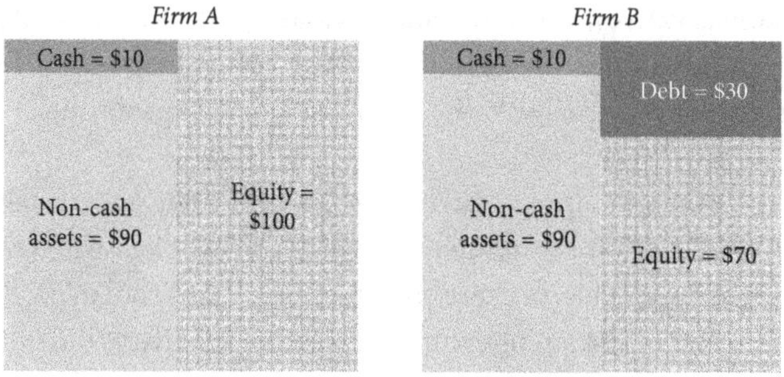

Figure 11.6 Example of two firms with different debt levels

The firm could alternatively restructure its debt in a *public workout*, that is, in bankruptcy court. But shareholders generally view bankruptcy to be undesirable because it will likely allocate most of the value to creditors and just leave some crumbs to shareholders.

In summary, debt payments create a strong commitment that can produce severe ripple effects, especially if the firm has defaulted on its payments or faces a debt overhang in which the firm value is less than the face value of the debt obligations. Figure 11.5 depicts how the ripple effects surge around defaults, accentuating the role of debt and default.

Consider the two firms in Figure 11.6 with different debt levels. Running out of cash is costly for firm A because it will have to constrain spending and likely suffer underinvestment. It might also have to sell some assets at fire-sale prices to free up some liquidity. Nevertheless, it can presumably keep on like that for a while.

Running out of cash is worse yet for firm B with its debt collectors hammering at the door. These debt collectors intensify the problem in that managers are forced to shift attention toward appeasing them, and the firm might have to default, thus triggering an array of new costs.

11.2 Debt payouts: Tax advantage

While debt can be treacherous due to its potentially large ripple effects, it comes with a great advantage: Unlike payouts to equityholders, the interest portion of debt payouts is deductible for tax purposes. A back-of-the-envelope calculation, based on the assumptions that (a) the interest payments represent a perpetuity and (b) the interest rate on debt is a reasonable approximation for the cost of capital for debt tax shields, gives the following:

$$Value\ of\ interest\ tax\ shield = \frac{Debt \times Interest\ rate \times Tax\ rate}{Interest\ rate}$$

$$= Debt \times Tax\ rate$$

This can easily be more than 10% of total firm value! Some would even argue that it dwarfs the expected ripple effects of having debt (i.e., the probability of incurring ripple effects times the costs of those ripple effects). In any event, the tension between the value of the interest tax shield and the ripple effects is what gives rise to the static trade-off theory and the accompanying optimal debt ratio. In fact, the graph in Figure 11.7 is presented in some form in just about all books on corporate finance. Note, however, that the ripple

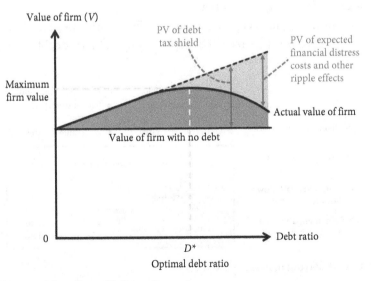

Figure 11.7 The effect of debt on firm value

effects from debt are generally called bankruptcy or financial distress costs in the context of capital structure, even though we have recognized that the ripple effects encompass more than what might be regarded as financial distress costs.

11.3 Revisiting the payout decision matrix

Equipped with our insight on debt payouts, we are ready to revisit the payout matrix. In Figure 11.8, I have added debt-financed payouts (also called *recaps*), in which firms take on more debt and pay out the proceeds to shareholders. Such debt-financed payouts have the effect of increasing the debt-to-equity ratio, but leave the assets, including the cash balance, intact. As a result, the firm is committed to pay out more funds in the form of interest and principal payments. This requires a strong and steady cash flow, and that is why the debt-financed payouts appear in the bottom row of the payout matrix.

I have also shaded the cells to indicate that these alternatives are tax-favored, and darker shading indicate greater tax benefits. Based on the shading, the best alternatives are on the lower and left part of the matrix, with a debt-financed repurchase providing the greatest tax benefits because it increases long-term debt tax shields in a way that minimizes the immediate tax penalty of the recap transaction.

If we are willing to accept the argument that repurchases are almost always favored from a tax perspective (especially those that are debt-financed),

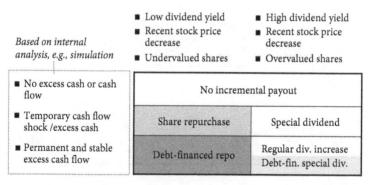

Figure 11.8 Payout matrix revisited

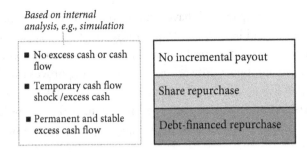

Figure 11.9 Simplified payout matrix

we could simplify our payout decision matrix further, making our payout decisions easier. Figure 11.9 shows the simplified payout matrix.

That got much easier, right? While it took some time to get here, we now have a more straightforward path toward the optimal payout (and capital structure) decision. Essentially all we must do is run a simulation to gauge the strength of our predicted future cash distributions. The stronger the distributions are, both in terms of magnitude and stability, the further down in the matrix we should move.

11.4 The use of convertible bonds

Convertible bonds allow bondholders to convert their bonds to a fixed number of shares. Thus, if the stock price were to increase substantially, a large portion of the bonds would likely be converted into equity.

Firms issue convertible bonds for a variety of reasons. For example, firms might include the convertibility feature in their bonds to comfort bondholders who might otherwise fear that the firm will act in a way to transfer value from bondholders to stockholders (see the section in Chapter 4 on the conflict between bondholders and stockholders). The convertibility feature might also be quite handy for managing a certain type of idiosyncratic risk. Let us see how.

Suppose that a firm faces the possibility of enhanced investment opportunities that would require substantial investments and funding. For example, a pharmaceutical company might have submitted an application to the Food and Drug Administration (FDA) to have a drug approved, and if the drug is approved, the company will have a lucrative, but expensive, opportunity to mass produce and launch the drug. In this situation, a convertible bond would alleviate the funding problem and facilitate the investment. If the lucrative investment opportunity arises (i.e., the FDA approves the drug), the capital market will applaud, and the stock price will increase. Consequently, the convertible bonds will be converted into equity, thereby reducing the burden of debt payments and freeing up debt capacity for the firm to raise more funds.

In short, the inclusion of a convertibility feature in bonds has the potential to provide firms greater financial flexibility precisely when they need it the most, especially for firms with uncertain investment opportunities that correlate with the stock price.

11.5 Some final words on debt financing and risk management

One way of thinking about the value of risk management is that it allows firms to take on more debt, thereby increasing the value of tax shields. If so, debt and risk management are complementary, and there should be a positive relation between financial leverage and risk management.

If risk management and debt are used in such a complementary way, we can create even more firm value than earlier parts of this book suggest. This emphasizes that risk management and financial policy should be considered simultaneously to maximize firm value.

In some cases, however, there is a hurdle to using risk management and debt as complements, because both the uses of derivatives and debt might require collateral, as mentioned earlier in the collateral dilemma section. If the collateral is limited, there is a potential trade-off between the uses of derivatives and debt, and derivatives and debt are substitutes instead of complements. The implication is that firms with heavy debt that is collateralized are more constrained in their risk management activities. That is, they can only resort to risk management that does not require collateral.

12

Wrapping Up

After many challenging chapters on risk management and corporate finance, it is useful to sit back and review some key insights. Here they are:

(1) A major goal for corporate managers is to ensure that the company has sufficient cash holdings to fund positive NPV investments and weather a storm. But we don't want so much cash holdings that the company becomes wasteful with its resources. We are like tourists on a cliff with a spectacular view; we want to get close to the edge so we can enjoy the view, but not so close as to endanger our lives. Just like Figure 12.1 shows.

(2) The primary tools to attain the goal above include risk management and payout policy, where payout policy might be extended to include payouts to both equity- and debtholders. There are two insights embedded here:

   a. The major reason for engaging in risk management is to ensure that the company has enough cash. That might be obvious to you now after having read this book, but if you ask risk managers how risk management creates value, you will get diverging answers and stumped expressions.

   b. Risk management and payout policy should be considered jointly; you might even treat them as substitutes in many situations. For example, a firm exposed to substantial risk but no effective risk management tools could instead resort to lower payouts.

(3) Risk can be difficult to identify and measure. We developed some helpful simulation tools for gauging how risk affects the cash distribution, but those tools hinge on our ability to make assumptions about how the risk factors affect various aspects of the operations, including sales volume, prices, competition, costs, and investment values. We also examined some regression tools that can assist in cases where both company and the risk factors are priced in the capital markets, such as a public airline and fuel prices.

Applied Corporate Risk and Liquidity Management. Erik Lie, Oxford University Press. © Oxford University Press 2023.
DOI: 10.1093/oso/9780197664995.003.0012

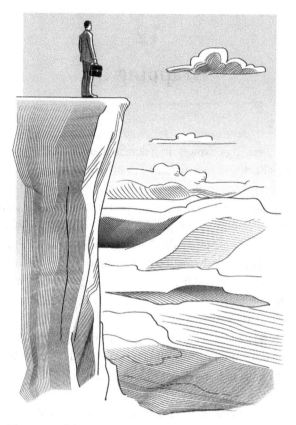

Figure 12.1 The view of an executive

(4) Risk can be difficult to mitigate. We discussed how firms tend to focus on commodity risk, which is possible to manage via derivatives. Systematic risk can also be managed via derivatives, but, oddly, most firms fail to do this. Idiosyncratic risk, which is generally the largest risk component, is difficult to manage, but fortunately we can still resort to lower payouts that will help protect the cash cushion.

(5) Among payouts, repurchases dominate because of superior flexibility and tax treatment. If a company can handle greater commitments because of strong and steady cash flow, it should consider taking on more debt. In our framework, dividends are never suitable.

References

Desmond, Matthew. 2016. *Evicted: Poverty and Profit in the American City*. Crown Publishers.

Froot, Kenneth A., David S. Scharfstein, and Jeremy C. Stein. 1993. "Risk Management: Coordinating Corporate Investment and Financing Policies." *Journal of Finance* 48 (5): 1629–58.

Lewent, Judy C., and A. John Kearney. 1990. "Identifying, Measuring, and Hedging Currency Risk at Merck." *Journal of Applied Corporate Finance* 2 (4): 19–28.

Index